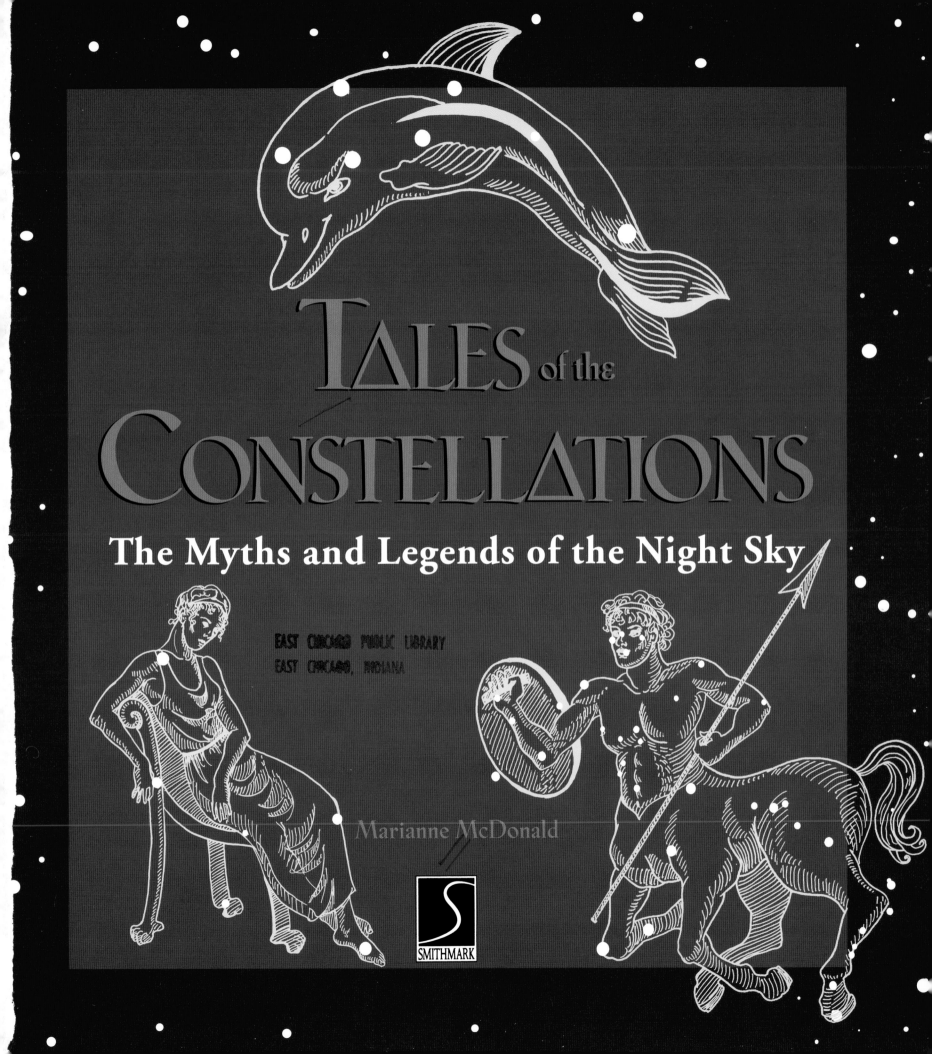

TALES of the CONSTELLATIONS

The Myths and Legends of the Night Sky

Marianne McDonald

SMITHMARK

A FRIEDMAN GROUP BOOK

Copyright © 1996 by Michael Friedman Publishing Group, Inc.

This edition published in 1996 by Smithmark Publishers,
a division of U.S. Media Holdings, Inc.,16 East 32nd Street,
New York, New York 10016

SMITHMARK books are available for bulk purchase for sales
promotion and premium use. For details write or call the manager
of special sales, SMITHMARK Publishers, 16 East 32nd Street,
New York, New York; (212) 532-6600

ISBN 0-8317-7277-8

TALES OF THE CONSTELLATIONS
The Myths and Legends of the Night Sky
was prepared and produced by
Michael Friedman Publishing Group, Inc.
15 West 26th Street
New York, New York 10010

Editor: Nathaniel Marunas
Art Director: Jeff Batzli
Designer: Andrea Karman
Photography Editor: Emilya Naymark
Line Illustrations: Emilya Naymark
Production Director: Karen Matsu Greenberg

Color separations by Fine Arts Repro House Co., Ltd.
Printed in Hong Kong and bound in China by Midas Printing Limited

Acknowledgments

The author would like to thank the following for their contributions to this book:

George Huxley, Bridget McDonald, and Thomas MacCary.

Contents

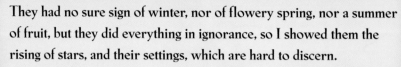

They had no sure sign of winter, nor of flowery spring, nor a summer of fruit, but they did everything in ignorance, so I showed them the rising of stars, and their settings, which are hard to discern.
(Aeschylus, *Prometheus Bound*).

This is the excellent foppery of the world, that, when we are sick in fortune often the surfeit of our own behaviour—we make guilty of our disasters the sun, the moon, and the stars....An admirable evasion of whoremaster man, to lay his goatish disposition to the charge of a star.
(Shakespeare, *King Lear*)

Study is like the heaven's glorious sun,
That will not be deep-searched with saucy looks.
Small have continual plodders ever won,
Save base authority from others' books.
These earthly godfathers of heaven's lights
That give a name to every fixèd star,
Have no more profit of their shining nights
Than those that walk and wot not what they are.
(Shakespeare, *Love's Labour's Lost*)

Men at some time are masters of their fates:
The fault, dear Brutus, is not in our stars,
But in ourselves, that we are underlings.
(Shakespeare, *Julius Caesar*)

The stars above us, govern our conditions.
(Shakespeare, *King Lear*)

He his fabric of the heavens
Hath left to their disputes, perhaps to move
His laughter at their quaint opinions wide
Hereafter, when they come to model Heaven
And calculate the stars, how they will wield
The mighty frame, how build, unbuild, contrive
To save appearances, how gird the sphere
With centric and eccentric scribbled o'er,
Cycle and epicycle, orb in orb.
(Milton, *Paradise Lost*)

Mystical dance, which yonder starry sphere
Of planets and of fixed in all her wheels
Resembles nearest, mazes intricate,
Eccentric, intervolved, yet regular
Then most, when most irregular they seem,
And in their motions harmony divine
So smoothes her charming tones that God's own ear
Listens delighted.
(Milton, *Paradise Lost*)

[Dionysus]
You, the lord of the dance of the fire-breathing stars,
The conductor of the voices of the night,.
Child sprung from Zeus, appear.
(Sophocles, *Antigone*)

Introduction

The Making
of Myths

OPPOSITE: THIS IS AN IMAGE OF SAHU, THE EGYPTIAN PARALLEL OF ORION; THE STARS OF THE BELT ARE SYMBOLICALLY RELATED TO THE THREE MAIN PYRAMIDS OF GIZA. A STAR MAP ILLUSTRATING THIS

CONSTELLATION WAS FOUND IN THE TOMB OF MONTEMHET AT LUXOR THAT DATES FROM AROUND 650 B.C.

Human beings have always been fascinated with the night sky, which is hardly surprising when one considers the beauty of the celestial pageant and the many practical uses to which the stars have been put. To explain the existence of these celestial bodies, humans have created myths of all descriptions—tales of love, hate, bravery, and cowardice—involving gods and heroes, animals and monsters, and various treasures.

The stars have always influenced human beings: early peoples planted their crops and navigated by the stars, and the earliest sciences and religions generally correlated with stellar observations. Early civilizations created mythologies to give meaning to the constellations and other astonishing phenomena of the universe. There is even a myth about the myths: Aeschylus' Prometheus tells us that he taught man the lore about the stars. Today, these tales tell us much about the inner and outer worlds both of human beings and of civilization in general. This book explores these worlds by recounting and comparing the tales that for countless generations people of diverse cultures have projected onto the constellations.

Myths, legends, parables or fables, folktales, and fairy tales all contribute to the lore of the stars. Myths serve many functions, from the sacred to the secular. The word *myth* derives from the Greek *muthos* and means "spoken word." Stories are handed down from generation to gen-

RA, THE SUN GOD, EMBARKS FOR HIS DAILY JOURNEY ACROSS EGYPT. THIS DRAWING IS A REPRODUCTION OF AN ILLUSTRATION FOUND ON AN ARCHITRAVE IN IDFU, WHICH WAS THE CAPITAL OF THE SECOND NOME, OR DISTRICT, OF UPPER EGYPT. IDFU IS THE SITE OF THE TEMPLE OF HORUS, A SANDSTONE STRUCTURE THAT IS BETTER PRESERVED THAN ANY OTHER LARGE ANCIENT EGYPTIAN BUILDING. MOST SURFACES OF THE TEMPLE ARE COVERED WITH INSCRIPTIONS THAT DETAIL BOTH THE ADMINISTRATIVE DETAILS OF ANCIENT EGYPT AS WELL AS ITS MYTHOLOGY.

eration, often told by parents to their children. They have many variations. Legends are grounded in history. Folktales are often humorous and entertaining, highlighting a clever human hero or heroine. The parable, or fable, teaches. In folktales, characters are often general types, rather than the individualized personalities of myth. Fairy tales are like folktales but involve the supernatural (if not the actual presence of fairies). The folktale is usually grounded in a specific time, whereas the myth tends to be timeless. Modern fantasies about the stars can be found in works of science fiction, from Asimov's *Foundation* trilogy to *Star Wars* and *Alien* to *No Escape*. One can see how all these categories overlap.

There are many types of myths, including the religious tale, the dream (wish-fulfillment) tale, the explanatory tale, and the entertaining tale. Obviously, these categories are flexible. Some myths endorse a claim or an institution; others are religious incantations meant to secure the status quo or to bring about change; some myths sublimate anxieties and assuage traumas; and still others are meant simply to amuse. Myths can order nature in human terms, allowing us to understand it better by identifying with it. Sometimes a myth is recited to exert control over nature—for instance, to ensure that the sun rises (in his nightly voyage, the Egyptian sun god, Ra, has to defeat the serpent Apophis in order to rise, and prayers were offered daily to help the god on his way). Myths are often associated with the supernatural, with gods, and with ritual. They

11

BOTH OF THESE COLOR-
FUL ENGRAVINGS COME
FROM CONSTELLATION
ATLASES OF THE EIGH-
TEENTH CENTURY AND
SHOW THE SKY FROM
THE SOUTHERN
HEMISPHERE, THOUGH
AT DIFFERENT SEASONS.
THE PROJECTED IMAGES
CLEARLY HAVE A WIDE
RANGE OF SOURCES,
FROM CLASSICAL GREEK
TO CONTEMPORARY
CHRISTIAN.

represent a sacred endorsement and are often used to legitimize peoples' claims to land or inheritance ("charter myths"). Many myths deal with death and the individual's place in the underworld. Fertility— of humans, animals, and land—is a frequent theme. Men and women also need to be organized and ranked in their activities and institutions, and myths can help impose social order. Myths can pose problems (and at times, solve them) or articulate (and in some cases, allay) human fears. They can appeal to the intellect and arouse feelings. Myths can be dreams that explore the meaning of life. As Prospero tells us, "We are such stuff /As dreams are made on, and our little life/Is rounded with a sleep" (*The Tempest*).

THIS TURN-OF-THE-CENTURY PAINTING BY ALEXANDRE SEON, *LAMENTATION OF ORPHEUS*, SHOWS THE LEGENDARY MUSICIAN CLUTCHING HIS LYRE, CLEARLY OVERCOME WITH GRIEF. THE MYTH OF ORPHEUS ILLUSTRATES BOTH THE POWER OF THE ARTS AND THE DEPTH OF HUMAN EMOTION.

Some would claim, as Jung did, that certain archetypes are common to all peoples. Joseph Campbell carried on a comparative study of mythologies and found many ties between them: he viewed heroic tales, for instance, as symbolic rites of passage a person must undergo to achieve a productive adult life. Sometimes Campbell errs by seeing too many similarities and forcing tales to fit his procrustean ideology, which is firmly rooted in Eastern philosophy. Sir James G. Frazer and Robert Graves also find unifying themes, such as fertility rituals and "the white goddess." Friedrich Max Mueller sees the sun behind every myth.

To explain similarities in myths, one could say that there is a universality in human perception

and imagination—perhaps because of human brain structure or because of common experiences—that led diverse cultures to develop the same myths independently. But there are many possible explanations for the similarities among myths. One could speculate that travelers at the dawn of civilization established links that are now forgotten. Perhaps it is obvious that humans should draw parallels between themselves and the universe in which they live, such as noting the reflection of the human cycle of life in the passing of the seasons. There is also the theory that some divine or supreme force in the universe has communicated these ideas (myths) to mankind. Perhaps it is simply a function of neural biology: some people claim

LIKE OTHER ASPECTS OF DAY-TO-DAY LIFE, FARMING WAS OFTEN RULED BY THE STARS. THIS FRENCH ILLUS-TRATION—A MONTH-BY-MONTH OVERVIEW OF FARMING ADVICE—IS PROBABLY FROM A TRANSLATION OF THE FAMOUS TWELVE-BOOK *OPUS RURALIUM COMMODORUM*, BY ITALIAN MEDIEVAL AGRI-CULTURALIST AND MAN OF LETTERS PIETRO CRESCENZI.

that humans share certain myths because of the bicameral structure of the human brain. Individual differences and needs, however, should not be minimized in these studies.

Human beings must define their status—not only their relation to one another, but to gods and animals and also to the heavens and the earth. Mythologizing helps define these relations. Not surprisingly, myths change with each telling, particularly if they are not written down (as is the case with most myths). Furthermore, these stories are often modified for specific reasons: to suit history, for instance, or to accommodate sacred influences involving cult and ritual. Besides the oral tradition itself, the literary tradition has

THE MAKING OF MYTHS

altered myths as well. All these factors have a hand in altering myths over time.

Myths differ from land to land, and we learn from the comparison of cultures the ways in which myths can operate. Bronislaw Malinowski studied the myths of the Trobriand Islanders; Lévi-Strauss, the South American Indians; Clyde Kluckhohn, the Navajos; and the Cambridge school, including Jane Harrison, the Greeks. Each of these researchers is inclined toward an overarching theory that may work for the specific culture he studied, but often breaks down when applied to other cultures. Malinowski sees myths as inexplicable narratives having no explanatory function, instead serving as sacred stories that accompany rituals. Lévi-Strauss sees myths as a strategy for mediating between opposites, such as raw and cooked, fresh and rotten, high and low, old and young, or primitive and civilized (nature/culture). Lévi-Strauss emphasizes structure over content, and shows how myths can be understood better through juxtaposition with other myths than they can be understood in themselves.

ONE OF THE MOST IMPORTANT OF THE GREEK MYTHS, THE TALE OF ODYSSEUS' EFFORTS TO RETURN HOME AFTER THE TROJAN WAR HAS INFORMED THE ARTS THROUGHOUT THE CENTURIES. MANY SEE HIS JOURNEY AS A VOYAGE OF SELF-DISCOVERY, WHICH IS ONE OF THE DRIVING FORCES BEHIND MYTHOLOGIZING IN GENERAL. HERE, ODYSSEUS IS STRAPPED TO THE MAST OF HIS BOAT AS THE SIRENS TEMPT HIM WITH THEIR SONG. THIS IS A DETAIL FROM A ROMAN MOSAIC THAT DATES FROM THE THIRD CENTURY A.D.

Lévi-Strauss disagrees with E. Durkheim, who sees myths expressing the collective ideas of a social group. Paul Ricoeur objected to Lévi-Strauss' generalizing from the myths of North and South American Indian societies rather than from those of Semitic, Indo-European, or Mediterranean areas. The myths Lévi-Strauss investigated often confused the human and the animal, exhibiting totemism in contradistinction to myths that centered upon anthropomorphic or abstract gods. Ricoeur also pointed out that Lévi-Strauss used myths from countries that emphasized structure and arrangement over content (they were based on *bricolage*, or assembling the things they found at hand rather than choosing objects or subjects that would convey a predetermined meaning). Lévi-Strauss also claims that a myth consists of all its versions, not taking note of the historical changes that can radically alter the meaning and significance of a myth. Thorkild Jacobsen saw the myths of Sumeria as concerned with creation, organization, and evaluation: one learned about gods, man, and the structure of the universe.

The mythical stage can also precede or contribute toward the scientific. As F. M. Cornford has said, "After the primitive stage of genuine myth-making, there is a transitional period, in which the old images and symbols are retained, but with a nascent consciousness that they do go beyond the meaning proper....Finally there may come a time when rational thinking consciously asserts itself, and the foremost intellects of the race awaken out of the dream of mythology....This happened in sixth-century Ionia, and what the Western world calls philosophy or science was born."

Kluckhohn and the Cambridge school saw an essential relationship between myths and rituals: the *legomenon* was the myth (what was said) and the *dromenon* was what was done (the ritual). Rituals could be rites of passage that enabled a person to leave one stage in his or her existence and go on to another, usually by means of isolation from the community and a series of tests. Or there could be rituals to ensure fertility, sometimes involving a sacrifice or payment to a god. The Cambridge school also spoke of the Year-Spirit, which clearly implied the change of seasons that coincided with the spirit's life, death, and rebirth. Myths can also be interpreted as star maps. For instance, the Mesopotamian Gilgamesh epic can be seen as representing the yearly transit of the sun through the constellations of the zodiac (obviously, it is the earth that moves, but for centuries it was thought that the sun itself traveled along a yearly path). There are also psychological interpretations

THIS FIFTH CENTURY B.C. GREEK URN (CALLED A *PELIKE*) ILLUSTRATES ONE OF THE MOST PREVALENT OF EARLY RITUALS, THE BLOOD SACRIFICE. IN THIS DETAIL, A BULL IS BEING LED TO THE ALTAR, WHICH IS SURROUNDED BY A MIXED COMPANY OF PRIESTS AND DEITIES.

of myths, as we find handed on by Karl Kerenyi, who is influenced by Jung, or Philip Slater, who shows a Freudian bias. Freud claimed that all myths were symbolic. The "unconscious" can shape myths, and Freud saw this as the "unconscious" of the individual, whereas Jung saw it as that of the race.

All these theories are useful, but one should be careful not to take one system of interpretation as absolute. We should paraphrase Lévi-Strauss and say that the proper interpretation of a myth consists of all interpretations. It is obvious, however, that in some cases one interpretation fits a particular myth better than another. The Freudian interpretation of the myth of Oedipus is more satisfying than the structural analysis of the same myth proposed by Lévi-Strauss, but both are interesting. Freud's association of the myth of Oedipus with the Primal Horde that first assassinated "the father" as the first act in an elaborate rite of passage does ask the average person to make a leap of faith. Also, the last thing that the ancient mythical Oedipus wanted to do was marry his mother, but Freud took the story to signify a universal drive of man to mate with his mother. To Freud, the myth of Electra describes the complex relationship between a daughter and a father. Once again, his interpretation is an extrapolation of the myth, which shows a daughter interested in seeing that her murdered father is avenged. Freud took myths and used them like a grammar, a framework for the meaning that he wanted to convey.

15

16

Ernst Cassirer focuses on the language of myth that is symbolically used to translate mythic thought. He also takes over L. Levy-Bruhl's idea of a primitive mentality (*la mentalité primitive*). According to this view, one becomes possessed, and myths write themselves. As he says, "The primitive mentality does not invent myths, it *experiences* them."

Many American Indian cultures view myths as dreams. Author Carlos Castenada writes about "dreaming" as something essential for a warrior, the ideal of the living human being. These dreams are like waking myths, sacred keys to a second reality. Similarly, Australian aborigines also speak of "Dreamtime" as an intensification of the present (consider Calderón's play *La Vida es Sueño* [Life Is a Dream]). It is also worth noting the Hindu creation/reincarnation myth of the god Vishnu

THEORISTS OFTEN USE THE DREAM AS A MODEL FOR THEIR STUDIES OF MYTHS, MANY OF WHICH INCORPORATE THE DREAM—AS ORACLE, MEDIUM, OR GENERATIVE FORCE. THIS SEVEN-TEENTH-CENTURY MINIATURE DEPICTS VISHNU DREAMING THE COSMIC DREAM. HE AND HIS WIFE, LAKSHMI, ARE ON THE BACK OF AN ANANTA BETWEEN TWO PERIODS OF COSMIC EVO-LUTION, DESTRUCTION AND CREATION.

dreaming the universe dream as he rides on the cosmic serpent who floats on the Milky Ocean.

Through dreams, one can sometimes approach the truth more clearly than through rational thought. Accordingly, the myths of a given culture should be taken as seriously as that culture's philosophic and scientific canons. Even if these tales do not necessarily contain cosmic truths, at least they can yield important information about a people.

Astronomy is an ancient science. The Egyptians practiced astronomy as early as the third millennium B.C. Soon, the movements of the stars were associated with human activity, and astrologers started to predict what would happen to humans based on the places the stars occupied in the sky. In many cultures, various predictions, both scientific and fanciful, were made based on the movements of the heavenly bodies. Thales of Miletus is said to have shown his astronomical prowess in predicting an eclipse in 585 B.C. Already in the works of Homer (c. 900 B.C.) some constellations are mentioned: Pleiades, Hyades, Bear/Wagon, Orion with his dog. According to Plato, the Greeks gave the name of their gods to five planets in the fifth century B.C., which in their Latin form are Jupiter, Saturn, Mars, Mercury, and Venus (their Babylonian equivalents are, respectively, Marduk, Ninib, Nergal, Nebo, and Ishtar). As other planets were discovered, they were given names of more gods in the Greek and Roman pantheon (e.g., Uranus, Neptune, and Pluto). The etymology of *planet* yields "wanderer." Perhaps the mobility of the planets led to this use of the gods' names for the planets; divine beings, more than any others, after all, have the ability to come and go as they wish. Western culture has given mainly Latin or Latinate Greek names to the planets, and Greek names to the constellations; Arabic names are mainly given to individual stars.

A myth can be a profound prayer, or it can be a simple wish. A star led the shepherds to Bethlehem to find Jesus Christ. For years humans have cast horoscopes based on the stars; if one is born under a certain constellation, one is said to have certain characteristics and to experience life events influenced by planetary movements. The Babylonians worshiped the sun, moon, planets, constellations, and stars. It was easy to infer from the regularity of the movement of the heavenly spheres that humankind was controlled by some outside force. This enhanced the idea of fate (and even necessity) governing a person's life. Obviously, if one could foretell life's events, then one had great power.

THIS CHINESE WATER-
COLOR SHOWS AN
ASTRONOMER AND HIS
EQUIPMENT, WHICH
INCLUDES AN ASTROLABE
AND TELESCOPE.

As we stand on earth looking at the night sky, from most places we can see about five thousand stars (probably closer to two thousand, actually). There are about seven thousand that we could potentially see if we could travel around the earth. In the Milky Way, there are about four hundred billion stars, and in the entire universe as we know it about one hundred billion billion stars. So we see only a small fraction of our galactic surroundings. As we have discussed, people of most cultures have been devising stellar ordering systems for millenia, right up until the present day. E.C. Krupp notes that in 1928 there were eighty-eight constellations accepted by the International Astronomical Union. The Chinese have different sets of stars, numbering twenty-eight, called *Sieu*, through which the moon passes each month.

Hesiod (c. 700 B.C.) certainly spoke of the birth of the universe in his *Theogony*, and in *Works and Days* he gives an almanac of favorable and unfavorable days. His lost *Astronomia*, which gave the risings and settings—and possibly myths—of the stars only survives in a few fragments. Eudoxus in the fourth century B.C. gives us an account of some of the signs of the zodiac, and some of the names of the planets. Aratus (270 B.C.) supplies more such information in his *Phainomena*. A generation later, Eratosthenes fills in the associated myths in the *Katasterismoi*, a work that was condensed by Pseudo-Eratosthenes, who wrote two to three centuries later. The Greek Stoics (from about 300 B.C.) prized star lore. They believed in fate and that the whole universe was organized in a cosmic unity. The Persians also believed in astral divinity.

17

Astrologers abounded in ancient Rome. In the first century A.D. it was a capital offense in Rome to cast the emperor's horoscope without the emperor's explicit authorization. Beginning in the second century A.D. Roman emperors were identified with the sun. Hyginus' *Poetica Astronomica* deals with some of the lore. Astrology continued to be popular during the Byzantine period, and Averroes (twelfth century) also considered it of scientific value, as did the thirteenth-century English philosopher Roger Bacon. Pope Leo X (sixteenth century) established a chair of astrology in Rome. By 1650 the belief in astrology diminished, at least in part because of scientific observations by Galileo, the development of a scientific method (based on observation rather than faith) by Francis Bacon, and the rationalist philosophy of René Descartes. Not surprisingly, the Enlightenment was a difficult time for the followers of astrology, but the practice nonetheless survived. As soon as new planets were discovered (Uranus in 1781 and Neptune in 1846), their influences were incorporated into astrological lore. There is a London Faculty of Astrological Studies that is world-renowned. From the many astrological publications alone, it is obvious that this science is alive and well. (Indeed, Nancy Reagan conducted her life according to astrology's dictates, and no doubt influenced her husband while he was president of the United States.)

Some people also wanted their religious beliefs confirmed by the stars, and thus rewrote the ancient text of the heavens. This process is a reflection of the ways in which ascendent cultures have established ownership and dominion through the renaming of conquered territories, religions, and even

ARATUS OF SICYON WAS AN EARLY ASTRONOMER WHO CONTRIBUTED TO THE POPULARITY OF STAR MYTHOLOGIES.

ideas. In Utah, the rock formations called The Four Apostles by the agents of Christendom had been given entirely different names by the regional Native American populations. The Irish had their own Gaelic place names, but these were brushed aside by the conquering Britons and replaced with English names to ensure domination (well commemorated in Brian Friel's play *Translations*). New stories and renamings often accompany a shift in power, and are a way for the new regime to dominate. One way to rule is to rewrite history, and the heavens were not immune to this phenomenon.

Myths deal with mankind's most profound concerns, desires, and fears, including (but not limited to) life and death and the individual's place in the universe. Indeed, some myths constitute an attempt to transcend the mortal coil. Although death is a sentence with no appeal, at least stories that tell of eternal life—or stories that are themselves eternal—allow human beings to take their place in the heavens, next to the gods in the form of constellations.

Heroes and heroines were frequently elevated to the stars, usually for having accomplished some exceptional deed—or many such deeds, as Heracles did. Great actions in themselves can be a source of eternal fame, but *katasterism*, or elevation to the stars, was the Nobel prize of heroism. But such immortalization can also be a punishment: the wrongs of Cassiopeia were punished by the inversion of her image in the heavens, thus making her appear ridiculous. Beside heroes, we also find among the constellations animals and monsters, and such things as a crown, a lyre, or a humble casserole in the heavens. All the objects associated with human beings can benefit from divine translation.

This book is an examination of the similarities and differences among different cosmologies. The text cites twenty-seven of the primary Greek constellations, using them as the starting point for a discussion of the related constellations of other cultures from around the world. Interestingly, many cultures picked out the same constellations, and some even interpreted those star groupings in the same way. For instance, the seven (or six) stars of the Pleiades represent seven (or six) young girls in several cultures, from

THE STARS OF THE PLEIADES ARE A GOOD EXAMPLE OF HEAVENLY PHENOMENA THAT HAVE BEEN INTERPRETED SIMILARLY BY SEVERAL CULTURES, MANY OF WHICH SAW THEM AS REPRESENTING A GROUP OF YOUNG WOMEN (AS DID THE JAPANESE).

Greece to Australia. Other constellations are interpreted differently by different cultures: the three bright stars that make up the belt of Orion from Greek mythology are Freya's spinning wheel of Scandinavian legend.

What do the stars tell us about the similarities and differences among the world's peoples? This will be the major thrust of this investigation. We shall concentrate on Greek myths because in the Western world, the Greek influence is at the foundation of many areas of cultural expression,

20

from art and literature to philosophy and medicine. Additionally, the Greek mythological canon is the largest and most complete such compendium of thought about the human condition that any people has ever produced, and it has been inscribed on the stars.

Similarities among star myths probably occurred when diverse peoples came into contact with one another or when the shape of a certain star formation was so suggestive that it inspired a particular interpretation. In general, however, different cultures developed different constellation myths—for any number of reasons, including geographic, economic, political,

THIS EGYPTIAN ZODIAC, WHICH DEPICTS THE NORTHERN CONSTELLATIONS AND SEVERAL PLANETS, ILLUSTRATES HOW IMPORTANT THE STARS WERE TO EARLY CULTURES. IT IS AMONG THE MOST FAMOUS PORTIONS OF THE TEMPLE OF HATHOR, ONE OF THE BEST-PRESERVED OF ANCIENT EGYPTIAN MONUMENTS.

or religious. For instance, seafaring nations of antiquity had a full complement of star myths, just as did civilizations that survived by farming. These canons differed according to the functions of the myths: the former depended on the stars for plotting voyages, and the latter used the stars to determine when to plant and when to harvest. Merchants had their own myths as well. The shapes the various constellations assumed also differed: sailors saw the Big Dipper as a ship; farmers saw it as a plow; and merchants saw it as a wagon. In the Arabic tradition, which emphasizes strictly observed rituals, the Big Dipper is seen as a funeral pro-

cession (the dipper part is the coffin). In China, where the emphasis is on communal harmony, the Big Dipper is *Ten Li,* or "Heavenly Reason." Obviously, there will be differences in the myths of a country that experienced yearly flooding and was structured around a hierarchy of kings and gods (Egypt, for example) and one that had a more regular supply of rain and was more democratic (such as Greece). The reasons for the differences in these traditions are many.

Greek myths have their own defining characteristics, with an emphasis on heroes and a tendency to underline the rational element. The Greeks put themselves at the center of the uni-

THESE MASKS, REPRESENTATIONS OF THE MOON (LEFT) AND SUN (RIGHT), WERE PROBABLY USED IN THE DLUWULAXA SOCIETY DANCE RITUALS, PERFORMED BY THE KWAKIUTL INDIANS OF NORTHWEST AMERICA TO CALL THE HEAVENLY BODIES TO EARTH.

verse, and thus did not place abstractions in the heavens; instead, they placed there gods, heroes, and the animals associated with both. In addition to mythological stories, the Greeks gave scientific explanations for movement in the universe. Many Native American Indians had matriarchal societies (for instance, the Ajumawi band of Pit River Indians of northeastern California), and in their myths the sun is female and the moon is male The ancient Japanese worshiped the goddess of the sun, Amaterasu, reflecting how, in the early history of the culture (before the militaristic Tokugawan regime came to power), women had a large degree of power.

22

One of the most famous Japanese epics, the *Tale of Genji* (twelfth century), is by Lady Murasaki. The Karraru aborigines of South Australia also claim that the sun is a woman, the Sun Mother who created life as she walked. Patriarchal societies favor a male sun god, and in some societies male rulers trace their lineage from the sun: the Chinese emperor is the son of heaven; Egypt's pharaoh is the son of the sun; and the Inca dynasty in Peru is descended from the sun. The Sumerians depict Shamash, the sun god, overcoming Siduri, the goddess of knowledge; Shamash takes over Siduri's powers and forces her to become a slave and work in a tavern.

ABOVE: THIS NINE-TEENTH-CENTURY WOODBLOCK PRINT BY UTAGAWA KUNISADA ILLUSTRATES THE SUN GODDESS AMATERASU AS SHE SHINES IN GLORY OVER THE COUNTRY OF THE RISING SUN, JAPAN. OPPOSITE: THIS FRENCH ENGRAVING IS A ROMANTICIZED DEPICTION OF CHINESE ASTRONOMERS AT WORK.

The human race has traditionally written its story in the heavens, sometimes even using an existing body of myths as the components of the narrative. As Seamus Deane says in a poem, "Homer Nods":

And could it be
We have here an autobiography
Pretending to epic for authority?
Protean creature, who has come to be
The proof that greatness lives vicariously
In the lies swapped round from men to God.
And when we hear the truth,
Not subject naturally, to proof,
We allow for Homer and we let him nod.

Tales of the

Constellations

΄Ανδρομέδα

ANDROMEDA

Our stories begin with the Greek tale of Andromeda, a beautiful woman clad only in jewels, chained to a remote rocky cliff in Joppa (Phoenicia), or possibly Philistia or Ethiopia. Some accounts say Andromeda had pale white skin, while others claim she was a black woman with flashing brown eyes and long black hair. Brutally chained to the rock, she would arouse sympathy in the most hard-hearted viewer.

Andromeda was the child of Cassiopeia and Cepheus. Cassiopeia had the temerity to boast that she was more beautiful than any of the

OPPOSITE:

ANDROMEDA IS RESCUED BY PERSEUS, WHO CARRIES MEDUSA'S HEAD IN A SACK AND WEARS THE HELMET OF HADES, MAKING HIM INVISIBLE. THE HERO RIDES PEGASUS, THE WINGED HORSE BORN FROM MEDUSA'S SEVERED NECK. THIS PAINTING IS BY GIUSEPPE CESARI.

Nereids (fifty sea nymphs, or mermaids). The Nereids went to their father, Poseidon, and asked for vengeance, which was quick in coming. Poseidon sent a huge female sea monster that devastated the country. (One way to demonize the female is to make her into a savage monster; this justifies control by the civilized [unmonstrous] male.) Cepheus consulted an oracle about how to bring the crisis to an end and received a dire message: he would have to offer his child as a sacrifice to the monster. Thus came Andromeda to be chained to the rock.

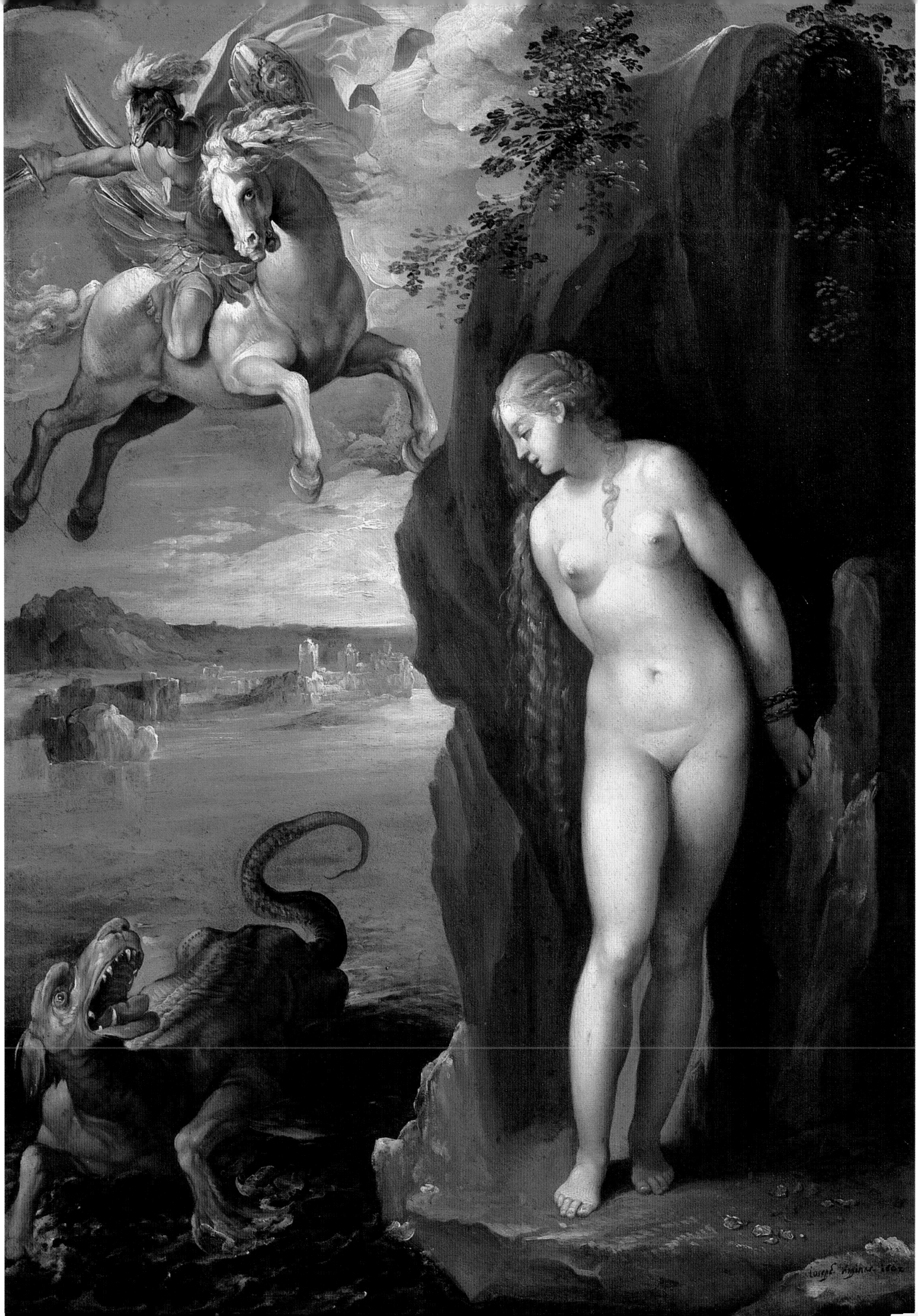

The hero Perseus was flying to the island of Seriphos, having accomplished his mission of slaying the Gorgon Medusa, when he saw the beautiful maiden, bound and helpless. He immediately fell in love with the young woman. He consulted with the king and queen and asked them what had to be done to release her; he also asked that she be given him in marriage. The royal couple agreed: provided he could slay the sea monster, Andromeda would be his.

Medusa's face turned all who saw it to stone. Perseus carried it in a *kibisis*, or wallet, that kept it out of sight (rather like a gun holster). When the sea monster came lumbering up, Perseus took out the deadly head and held it up, turning the horrible creature into stone. Perseus put the Medusa head on the shore facedown, and it transformed the immediate ecology: the seaweed spattered with the monster's blood turned into the blood-orange coral that is now so famous throughout the Mediterranean.

What Perseus did not know yet was that the double-crossing queen had already promised Andromeda's hand to Agenor (some say Phineus, Cepheus' brother) and was not going to give Andromeda away to a perfect stranger, however heroic. The queen encouraged Agenor, who arrived with an armed retinue, to kill Perseus. But Perseus had the Gorgon's head, and with it he turned Agenor and his army—along with the king and queen—into stone, then flew off with his hard-won bride. They had many children. Perseus himself gave his name to the Persians, and one son was named Perses.

There are several parallel stories within Greek mythology. In one tale, the gods Apollo and Poseidon were hired by Laomedon to erect the walls of Troy. Laomedon agreed to give the gods a fine wage, but reneged, so Poseidon set a sea monster loose to ravage the land. An oracle revealed that if Laomedon sacrificed his daughter Hesione, the land could be freed of the scourge. Heracles came by and saw the naked

Hesione chained to the rock. He said he would rescue her if her father would give her—in addition to some divine horses Laomedon owned—to him. Laomedon agreed and Heracles defeated the sea monster by letting the monster swallow him and then hacking his way out, killing the monster in the act of escaping. Laomedon reneged again (some people never learn). Heracles sacked Troy and seized the horses and Hesione. Since Heracles had sufficient amorous attachments himself, he gave her as a concubine (she paid the price of her father's treachery) to his good friend Telamon, to whom she bore the hero Teucer. Telamon was also the father of Ajax, whose mother was Eriboea.

This tale of a bound, vulnerable girl and her heroic rescue appeals to the imagination. The myth also fulfills a type of dream fantasy. The chained woman can be seen as a symbol of mastery over woman herself, a common archetype in patriarchal societies. The "Great Mother" is a psychological archetype that writers such as Erich Neumann *(The Great Mother)* and Karl Jung say is common to the human experience. Some theorists, including Robert Graves and Sir James Frazer, have posited that this expression stems from an original, ruling goddess of the Mediterranean region that was later ousted by patriarchal societies.

Andromeda, Virgo (not included in this book), and Cassiopeia are the only female constellations, so they have been identified with the Great Mother in her three aspects: maiden, matron, and crone (personified by Persephone, Demeter, and Hecate). Andromeda has been identified with Ishtar, Kore, and Persephone, the last a fertility goddess representing the seed. Persephone's season is winter, when the seed is nestled in the earth and when Persephone is visiting Hades. When she rejoins her mother, Demeter, in the spring it is time for the seed to sprout. The world rejoices when mother and daughter reunite.

The sixth-century B.C. poetess Sappho celebrates Andromeda, and the fifth-century B.C. playwrights Euripides and Sophocles wrote plays about her. Aristophanes, in the comedy called *Thesmophoriazousae*, depicts a relative of Euripides chained by the women on whose rites he was spying. The Peeping Tom recites verses from Euripides' play *Andromeda* in hopes that Euripides will act as his Perseus and free him.

In India, this constellation was called Antarmada, and there is a Sanskrit manuscript that has drawings of Capuja (Cepheus), Casyapi (Cassiopeia), and Antarmada with a fish close by (Pisces); Parasica (Perseus) is in evidence as well, holding a head that has serpents for hair. It is obvious that there was communication with the Greeks.

The Arabs called this constellation *al-Mar'ah al-Musalsalah,* "The Woman in Chains." They represented it by a chained seal since human representation was forbidden.

Julius Schiller (1627), who reinterpreted the constellations in Christian terms, called Andromeda *Sepulchrum Christi,* "the tomb of Christ." One wonders if he was influenced by the misogyny of the early Christian fathers, who saw woman as a snare for the pious man, and a source of the death of his soul. There is also the Freudian analogy, which associates cask with the woman. The fertility implications are obvious: Christ was in a tomb, waiting to rise again (like Tammuz or Osiris)—the seed ready to emerge in the spring.

The star called *Gamma Andromedae,* or *Alamac,* comes from the Arabic *al-Anak al-Ard,* which

means "badgerlike animal." There are other names given to it that mean "The Fifth of the Ostriches" and "Foot of the Woman." The Chinese called it *Tien Ta Tseang,* "The Great General of the Sky." In Hebrew lore Andromeda was Abigail, the wife of David, as related in the Book of Samuel.

The Phoenicians, a maritime people famous for lumber and colored textiles, were said to equate this constellation with a threshing floor and, alternately, a person harvesting in a field of wheat.

The Andromeda myth illustrates mankind's ability (personified by Perseus) to overcome nature (in the form of the two monsters). Perseus killed two female monsters: Medusa, a monster of the earth, and Cetus, a sea monster. The chained Andromeda, suspended in space, can be considered a creature of the air. Thus, man has overcome, or tamed, the female, who represents nature: the earth, the seas, and the sky. A natural subject for the operatic stage, there have been several such treatments of this myth, beginning with Francesco Manelli's *Andromeda* (1637), the first opera to be performed before a paying audience. Andromeda was later the name given to a hypothetical virus that would destroy the human race, in Michael Crichton's *The Andromeda Strain.*

Andromeda, a wild creature to be tamed and harnessed to creative—rather than destructive—ends, has haunted the imagination of the West for centuries.

29

CASSIOPEIA

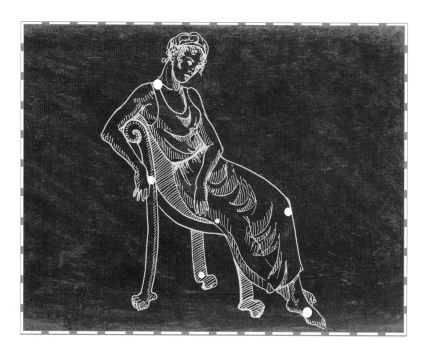

Andromeda's mother, Cassiopeia, and father, Cepheus, are also placed in the heavens. Cassiopeia was the daughter of Arabus (whose name was given to Arabia), a son of Hermes. She was prideful and willful, qualities for which her innocent daughter—and the bridegroom who rescued her—suffered. It is said that whereas Athena put Andromeda in the heavens as a reward, Poseidon put Cassiopeia there as a punishment (by special request of the Nereids). Cassiopeia is seated in a chair that turns upside down in each twenty-four-hour cycle; she is tied to the chair so that she will not fall out (or to keep her prisoner). Whereas

OPPOSITE: HECATE IS AN OLDER GODDESS WHO REPRESENTS MATURITY IN THE TRIAD OF GODDESSES THAT INCLUDES PERSEPHONE AND DEMETER. HECATE'S POWERS ARE SOMEWHAT MYSTERIOUS, AS SUGGESTED IN THIS LATE-EIGHTEENTH-CENTURY PAINTING BY ENGLISHMAN WILLIAM BLAKE.

her daughter was briefly tied because of her mother's vanity, Cassiopeia is tied for all eternity. The daily inversion makes the vain queen look ridiculous, a fate worse than death for one who prided herself on her beauty so much that she challenged the immortal Nereids (and some say even Hera) with her boasting. In Cassiopeia we have the wicked queen from *Snow White*, a frequent archetype in folktales. She wants to be worshiped and will not tolerate a rival. Such all-consuming egotism can be destructive for a daughter.

Cassiopeia can also be seen as Hecate, or the harvested grain. As an older goddess, Hecate is

the queen and leader of the abovementioned triad that includes Andromeda, or Persephone, the maiden; and Demeter, the mother. Hecate's destructive quality existed alongside her creative one (one parallel is the Indian goddess Parvati, identified with the fertile womb, or *yoni*, one of whose avatars is Kali the destroyer). Cassiopeia is often represented carrying a palm frond, a symbol of fertility. We remember Demeter depicted as giving grain to Triptolemus.

Schiller sees Cassiopeia as Mary Magdalene, both of whom he considered "uppity women." Some see a parallel between Cassiopeia and Bathsheba. Other interpreters, who are not thrilled by Mary Magdalene's—or Bathsheba's, for that matter—colorful past, symbolically replace her with the chaste Deborah.

The main stars in Cassiopeia have Arabic names, the meanings of which are "breast," "hand," "hump of the camel," "knee," and "elbow." They call the entire constellation "seder tree."

Some saw this constellation in the shape of a key. The Arabs called it *Al Dhat al Kursiyy*, or the "Lady in the Chair" (probably the result of communication with the Greeks), but earlier Arabs thought this was "the large hand stained with henna," the brightest stars glowing on the fingertips.

THIS MOSAIC OF CASSIOPEIA DATES FROM AROUND THE SECOND CENTURY B.C. AND WAS FOUND NEAR THE TEMPLE OF BEL (A SYRIAN GOD) IN PALMYRA, AN ANCIENT SYRIAN OASIS CITY.

Other cultures saw Cassiopeia and Cepheus as two dogs.

The Celts called this constellation *Llys Don*, "the home of Don," a fairy king and father of Gwydyon. The Chinese called it *Ko Taou*, relating it to a porch-way; its main star, Wang Liang, was a prominent charioteer of about 470 B.C. The Egyptians saw the constellation as a leg.

CETUS

The sea monster that attacked Andromeda has been identified as Cetus and is located near her constellation. The original Cetus, or Ceto, of myth is the daughter of the sea (Pontus) and the earth (Gaia). Cetus gave birth to the Graeae, the Gorgons, Echidne, the Hesperides, and Ladon, the hundred-headed dragon that stood watch over the apples of the Hesperides. Cetus is often shown with a greyhound's head and legs, and a trident's tail. Cetus is sometimes represented as closely resembling a whale, and sometimes a dolphin with protruding tusks. It is related to Draco, Hydra, and Serpens, which are all snakelike monsters.

The Arabs separated this constellation's stars into distinct groups: "The Part of a Hand," "Hen Ostriches," and "The Necklace." Biblical parallels are Jonah's whale and Leviathan from the Book of Job.

Cetus' main star, Mira, meaning "wondrous," is a red star that pulsates, changing in size and brightness over a period of 331 days. Thus, its light is seen to increase and decrease. Finally, Mira is located in the neck of Cetus and has been called the constellation's necklace.

Some stars close to Mira were called *Tien Hwan* by the Chinese, meaning "heaven's sewer." Even a sewer can shine brightly if it runs through the heavens.

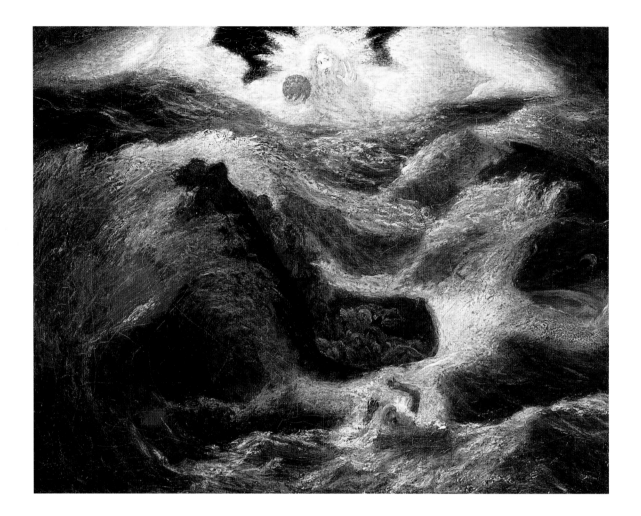

Cetus/Ceto is also identified with Tiamat. This was the female monster that Marduk overcame to create the universe. He split her into the heavens and into the earth. He assigned Anu the heavens, Enlil the earth and the atmosphere, and Ea the waters. The Babylonian creation epic, *Enuma Elish*, goes on to say that the constellations were made in the likenesses of the gods.

Cetus is woman as monster, a strange being that destroys as much as she creates, though she mainly creates other monsters. In a way, she is Cassiopeia's vanity incarnate, her flaw made manifest as a monster, perhaps a

THIS LATE-NINETEENTH-CENTURY PAINTING BY ALBERT PINKHAM RYDER DEPICTS THE EVENTS THAT BEFELL JONAH, WHO WAS DEVOURED BY THE WHALE (THE CHRISTIAN CETUS).

strange doublet of the queen. It is worth noting that in Greek mythology, many of the monsters are female. This may reflect the cultural aftermath that occurred when the mother goddesses who had ruled in Asia and Crete before the arrival of the Greeks were replaced by the latter culture's patriarchal gods. Just as Christians transformed pagan spirits called *daimones* into demons, and Venus, the morning star (which also sets and becomes the evening star), also called Lucifer ("the bearer of light"), into an eponym for Satan, so may the Greeks have transformed Cetus from a mother goddess into a monster.

Πήγασος

PEGASUS

Sirrah, the star that flashes from Andromeda's head in the constellation that bears her name, is also one of the four stars that make up the square in the constellation of Pegasus. This famous winged horse sprang from Medusa's neck—along with Chrysaor, the warrior who carries a golden falchion (curved sword)—when Perseus cut off the Gorgon's head. Pegasus and Chrysaor were the offspring of Poseidon, with whom Medusa mated in Athena's temple, violating the goddess' sacred precinct. This violation was particularly severe because Athena prided herself on being a virgin (the Parthenon, or the "place of the virgin," was named for her).

Pegasus' name may come from the Greek *pêgê*, or "spring." These springs were ocean springs in the far western part of Greece, where Medusa was killed. Pegasus is associated with several springs. When the Muses and the Pierides competed in singing, Mount Helicon swelled with its enjoyment and was about to touch the heavens when Poseidon ordered his son Pegasus to strike the mountain, causing it to shrink to its normal size. Where Pegasus hit the mountain, a fountain sprang out and *Hippocrene*, or "Horse Spring," can be found there to this day. There is another spring at Troezen that was created the same way. Pegasus eventually became a servant of Zeus and was said to bring the god his lightning.

Another story depicts Pegasus drinking at the Pierian spring (*Hippocrene*, the spring created by Pegasus, which was beloved by the Muses), where Bellerophon caught and tamed him, some say with Athena's help. Pegasus enabled Bellerophon to slay the Chimera and defeat the Amazons.

The son of either Glaucus or Poseidon, Bellerophon killed a man, possibly called Bellerus (Bellerophon means "slayer of Bellerus"), and he went to King Proetus, the ruler of Tiryns, to be purified of the murder he had committed. Proetus' wife, Sthenoboea, tried to seduce Bellerophon, and when he refused she falsely told Proetus that he had made unwelcome advances, knowing full well that the young man would suffer dire consequences. (There are many parallel stories featuring such predatory women—including Phaedra and Hippolytus, Astydamia and Peleus, and Demodoke and Phrixus—all of which are variations on the theme of the overt female monster. Needless to say, men were likely the authors of these tales.)

Proetus sent Bellerophon to Iobates, Proetus' father-in-law, the king of Lycia, with a secret written message that the young man should be killed. Bellerophon was sent to kill the Chimera in the hopes that he would die in the attempt. But he succeeded in defeating the beast, with the help of Pegasus. He was able to fly down on the Chimera, which had the forequarters of a lion, the hindquarters of a dragon, and a goat's head that emitted

BELOW: THIS MAGNIFICENT DETAIL IS TAKEN FROM A SIXTH-CENTURY B.C. CUP FOUND NEAR WHAT USED TO BE RHODES, ILLUSTRATING THE CONFRONTATION BETWEEN BELLEROPHON, WHO IS RIDING PEGASUS, AND THE CHIMERA.

OPPOSITE: LOCATED IN THE PALAZZO LABIA IN VENICE, THIS TRIUMPHANT CEILING PAINTING BY EIGHTEENTH-CENTURY MASTER TIEPOLO GIAMBATTISTA SHOWS PEGASUS CARRYING BELLEROPHON TOWARD GLORY, SURROUNDED BY AN ADMIXTURE OF CLASSICAL GREEK AND CONTEMPORARY FIGURES.

flames. He thrust a great lump of lead down the monster's throat, and the monster was strangled by the molten metal. Bellerophon was not even singed, and easily made his escape.

The king set Bellerophon many tasks, and in all he was successful. He was only defeated when a group of Xanthian women lifted their skirts and exposed their genitalia. They offered themselves to him; in his modesty, Bellerophon refused and stopped attacking their land (some versions say he turned and fled). The Xanthian king was so pleased with the resourcefulness of the women, he decreed that inheritance be reckoned through the mother. Bellerophon did defeat the armies of the Solymi and the Amazons. For this, Bellerophon earned Iobates' respect and was given the hand of one of his daughters—and the kingdom as well, after Iobates' death.

Success went to his head, however, and Bellerophon tried to ride Pegasus up to the home of the gods on Mount Olympus. Zeus sent a gadfly to sting Pegasus; the horse threw his rider and Bellerophon fell to earth. The fallen hero spent the rest of his life wandering alone, a bitter, crippled man.

There are many winged horses in Middle Eastern art, and these all may be related to this myth. Some say that the early Aryans claimed that this constellation represented Asva, the sun. Later

artists, including Shakespeare in *Troilus and Cressida*, associated Pegasus directly with Perseus, but the ancients did not. Some say that it was Chiron's daughter Thea whom we find in the heavens as the constellation of the horse, elevated there by Poseidon. She was a companion of Artemis, who was seduced by Aeolus, the god of the wind. Poseidon helped Thea avoid her father's wrath by turning her into the horse called Euippe.

The Greeks also identified the four stars in Pegasus (called the Square of Pegasus) as the gate to paradise for souls who escaped the necessity of reincarnation. The Hebrews called Pegasus "Nimrod's horse." Christians saw it as the ass that carried Christ into Jerusalem, commemorated by Palm Sunday. Schiller viewed it as the Archangel Gabriel. *Pagas* is the horse of the Aswin twins (who themselves are depicted with horse heads) in the sacred Hindu text, the *Rig Veda*. The horse is important in Vedic lore, and was sacrificed to ensure the favor of the gods.

The Egyptians identified this constellation as "The Servant," and some of its stars as a jackal. The Arabs called its quadrangle *Al Dalw*, or "water bucket," which has also been identified as the urn in the zodiacal constellation Aquarius. They also

TO CHRISTIANS, THE CONSTELLATION OF PEGASUS MAY REPRESENT THE ASS THAT JESUS RODE INTO JERUSALEM (COMMEMORATED NOW ON PALM SUNDAY) BEFORE HIS ARREST AND CRUCIFIXION.

call one of the stars *Markab*, which means "saddle," "ship," or "vehicle." One story tells us that Perseus built a ship called *Pegasus* that was said to sail as swiftly as the horse that flew.

The Chinese associate some stars of this constellation with *Ying She* (or *Shih*), which means "house," another *Luy Tien*, "thunder," and yet another *Jih*, "the sun."

By riding Pegasus and accomplishing his various tasks, Bellerophon is accomplishing a sort of wish fulfillment of the young hero. Bellerophon and Perseus, after they fly about and slay the monsters of their childhood, are able to enter into adult relations with women of their choosing (Bellerophon with Philonoe, the daughter of Iobates, and Perseus with Andromeda). In the end, Perseus was luckier: he got to keep his mother (he took Danae with him to Argos and Tiryns) and his fame, whereas Bellerophon died a broken man.

One can see these stories as rites of passage; in Freudian terms the winged horse is associated with the potent phallus (in ancient Greek art there were many representations of winged phalloi), with the aid of which it is possible for the adolescent boy to complete the difficult transition to manhood. The young hero has to prove himself before he can reap the fruits of life.

PERSEUS

The constellation of Perseus, the hero who rescued Andromeda, is close to the constellations of Andromeda, Cetus, Cassiopeia, and Cepheus. Perseus was the son of Danae, who was impregnated by Zeus in a shower of gold. The lusty god was forced to disguise himself in this manner because Danae's father had her locked up in a tower. (Rationalists see the shower of gold as a bribe to the jailer, the woman who was in charge of the keys.) Acrisius, Danae's father, was told that she would give birth to a son who would kill him, so he took precautions (which proved insufficient, as Danae's pregnancy grew more and more evident). After the birth, Acrisius locked mother and child in a chest and launched it into the sea. The chest washed up on the island Seriphos. There a fisherman, Dictys (whose name means "net"), pulled them ashore and protected them. His brother, Polydectes, ruler of the island, became enamored of Danae, but she refused him. Polydectes wanted to get rid of the grown (and therefore troublesome) Perseus, so he made a trap for the young man. He said he was going to get married and needed presents to impress the bride. Polydectes asked for horses, but Perseus was not able to provide such a gift and rashly offered anything in its stead. Polydectes asked for the head of Medusa.

Athena gave Perseus a shield polished to mirrorlike perfection, and Hermes gave Perseus a blade with which to cut off the head. The two gods told Perseus how he could acquire other useful tools. First he had to visit the Graeae, three old women who had one eye and one tooth among them. He stole their one eye and forced them to tell him where to find the Stygian nymphs who could give him what he needed. He found the nymphs and took from them winged sandals, a *kibisis* to carry the head in, and finally a helmet that made the wearer invisible.

Medusa had been a beautiful woman who was turned into a monster (either because she had compared her beauty with that of Athena or because she had been impregnated by Poseidon in a temple sacred to Athena). She had boasted particularly about her hair, so Athena made sure that it would be ugly, replacing the individual strands with hissing snakes. She was also transformed into a winged scaly monster with tusks and bronze hands. Her glance literally petrified onlookers (though ugly, she had a captive audience). Perseus slew her as he looked at her reflection in the shield Athena had given him, and some say that Athena guided his hand. Medusa's sisters, Stheno and Euryale, who were also Gorgons, flew to the attack, but Perseus put on the helmet of invisibility and flew off to

THIS HEROIC STATUE BY SIXTEENTH-CENTURY ITALIAN MASTER BENVENUTO CELLINI DEPICTS PERSEUS TRIUMPHANT, HOLDING ALOFT HIS DANGEROUS PRIZE, THE HEAD OF MEDUSA.

safety. (Charles Schneer's *Clash of the Titans* shows Medusa in all her snaky glory.)

Perseus then rescued Andromeda, but there were complications. Cassiopeia had promised her daughter to Phineus (in other versions Agenor), Cepheus' brother. Phineus tried to kill Perseus but Perseus held up the Gorgon's head and turned Phineus and his armed retinue to stone. He returned to Seriphos with Andromeda. They flew over the Libyan desert and some drops from the severed Gorgon's head fell down to the earth and turned into snakes: this is why Libya has so many snakes.

At Seriphos, Perseus rescued his mother, who was being blockaded there by Polydectes. He turned the grasping ruler into stone and gave the kingdom to the generous Dictys. Perseus returned his precious gifts to the gods and gave the head of Medusa to Athena to put in the middle of her shield, the *aegis*. He intended to return to Argos, but took part in some funeral games along the way, during which he threw a discus, accidentally killing his grandfather Acrisius and fulfilling the prophecy that Acrisius would be killed by his daughter's son (most oracles were devastatingly accurate). Mourning Acrisius' death, Perseus decided to rule Tiryns instead of Argos, and exchanged kingdoms with Megapenthes, son of Proetus.

40

Since Perseus gave his name to Persia, some have associated him with the Persian Mithras, the head of the martially oriented Mithraic religion so popular in the Roman army. Mithras was associated with Ahura Mazda, the god of light and goodness, who overcame Angra Mainyu, the god of darkness and evil. Mithras at first was the helper, but then he became the central figure in a cult that offered salvation through baptism in the blood of a bull and by following certain rituals. Mithras was born on December 25. The

BAROQUE MASTER MICHELANGELO CARAVAGGIO'S DAVID DISPLAYS THE SEVERED HEAD OF GOLIATH; THE WAY IN WHICH HE PRESENTS THE GRISLY REMAINS OF HIS ENEMY IS REMINISCENT OF THE DEPICTIONS OF PERSEUS AND HIS DEADLY TROPHY.

bull that Mithras slew was a source of life, and contained the seeds of creation in its body. When the bull was slain, wheat came from its spine, and its blood became the wine at services. One can see how this influenced Christianity: not only does Mithras share a birth date with Christ, but Christ at the Last Supper offered bread and wine saying, "This is my body and this is my blood." All these rituals commemorate the sowing and harvesting of grain and grape, the yearly cycle of life and death.

In Perseus' constellation he is seen holding a sword in one hand and in the other the head of Medusa, though there are other interpretations. Some see David holding the head of Goliath, and others the Apostle Paul with his sword and book. Because Saint George, the dragon slayer, was born at Lydda, which was close to Joppa (the site of the rescue of Andromeda), he is another candidate for this constellation.

The most famous star in this constellation is *Algol*, the demon that the Arabs call *Ra's al Ghul*, the "Demon's Head." This star is obviously Medusa's, which is sometimes interpreted with the Gorgon stars as a separate constellation, next to Perseus, of course.

Hebrews call this star *Rosh haatan*, or the Head of Satan. It has also been identified with Lilith, the temptress demon from the Old Testament who appears in Goethe's *Walpurgisnacht* as one of the evil spirits.

The Chinese also had an evil association with this star, which they called *Tseih She*, or "The Piled-up Corpses." It is regularly regarded as baleful, and changes shape in accordance with its unreliable nature.

This story, which encompasses the six constellations just discussed (including Cepheus), offers many interpretations to the psychologically inclined. Freud equated the Gorgon with the female genitalia. (Freud often noted a symbolic displacement of the genitalia upward to the head.) Since according to Freud women have penis envy, this myth shows her over-

SOME CULTURES ASSOCIATE THE CONSTELLATION OF PERSEUS WITH THE MESOPOTAMIAN GODDESS LILITH, DEPICTED IN THIS TERRA-COTTA RELIEF FROM AROUND 2000 B.C. AND DEMONIZED BY THE WRITERS OF THE OLD TESTAMENT.

compensation by developing a whole bunch of pseudo-penises. The head of snakes (female genitalia) that turns onlookers to stone might imply that the gazer develops a priapism. Philip Slater disagrees with this interpretation, saying the gazer suffers sexual paralysis. He interprets the whole story in terms of a boy possessing his mother. The father is absent, so the only threat to the child is his mother's own aggressive and resentful sexuality. Perseus/child kills Medusa/mother substitute, depriving her of her sexuality (cutting off her head/genitalia, the snakes as pubic hair). He tames his real mother (Danae, the mythical mother) by depriving her of a sexual partner (he locates her mateless in Tiryns). He also tames Andromeda by killing her aggressive side (the monster Cetus).

Much of this can be dismissed, but there are some themes that are relevant. I think Freud was correct in pointing out the strong connection between children and their parents, and that parents stimulate early sexual fantasies. He should have focused more on daughters, though: if there is penis envy, why not vagina envy? One cannot overestimate the importance of the mother in the early life of a child: a good, caring mother could be translated into a protecting goddess figure (Athena) and a jealous, aggressive mother could be a monster (Medusa). At any rate, one knows how a withering glance from a mother can turn a child to stone. The introduction of the feminine slant opens the door to a world of alternative interpretations.

'Αετός

AQUILA

This constellation is associated with Zeus' eagle, the one that carried off Ganymede. This eagle might be the form that Zeus himself took. There was a large bronze statue made by Leochares in the fourth century B.C. of this very incident, and we see Ganymede being carried off by the eagle, his face turned toward the eagle as if to kiss him. We have seen the eagle as a symbol of virility and power.

Aquila is in the area that the Sumerians particularly designated "the sky," and he shares this sector with other flying creatures, such as Pegasus. Indians say that Aquila brought to Indra soma, the drink that revived the Vedic god's energy for his yearly fight with the forces of darkness. Aquila was also known to the Greeks as the bird that brought rain (besides being a symbol of Zeus, the god of rain). The Arabs called this constellation al-Nasa-al-Tair, "The Flying Vulture," and the star Altair is so-named because of this. The Hebrews knew this constellation as Nesher, an eagle. The Christians called it "Saint Catherine the Martyr." Native Australians identify Aquila as Totyarguil, a mythical hero who met an untimely death while bathing in a lake; he was killed by a kelpie.

There are several myths associated with this constellation. The Chinese, Japanese, and Koreans all see the stars Altair (from Aquila) and Vega (Lyra) involved in a romantic story. She-niu was a modest girl who could weave extraordinary creations. She fell in love with a charming shepherd. They met each day by crossing a river that separated their lands. Fate intervened and the shepherd had to leave. She-niu waited faithfully for him to return until she died, still loving only him. He also died, remaining faithful always to her. The gods did not want such love to go unrewarded, so they transported the lovers to the heavens. The river that now separates the lovers is the Milky Way. The Weaver still weaves her colorful fabrics, and the Shepherd still tends his flocks, but they have been translated into stars. Once a year in early summer, on the seventh night of the seventh moon, the Shepherd joins the Weaver, and their stars shine brilliantly together. Magpies form a bridge on which the Shepherd can cross the Milky Way and join his beloved. When the magpies return home, they have lost the feathers on their head—the price for forming a bridge for the Shepherd. If it rains at night, the raindrops are tears of joy; if in the morning, they are tears of sorrow at parting. In Japan the festival commemorating this celestial romance is called Tanabata, when mortals dream of their true beloved during the one night when the star lovers meet. One can also tie wishes to trees to ask these divine lovers for help in matters of the heart. Appropriately, Aquila has been associ-

ABOVE: THIS HAUNTING ROMAN STATUE DEPICTS THE TRAGIC LOVER OF HADRIAN, ANTINOUS. OPPOSITE: MUCH HAS BEEN MADE IN THE ARTS REGARDING THE GIFT OF FIRE THAT PROMETHEUS BROUGHT TO HUMANITY; IN FACT, SOME PEOPLE HAVE POSITED THAT THE FLAME REPRESENTS THE CREATIVE IMPULSE ITSELF. WHETHER PRACTICAL OR SYMBOLIC, THE VALUE OF THE GIFT IS GREAT IF PROMETHEUS' PUNISHMENT IS ANY GAUGE. THIS NINETEENTH-CENTURY DEPICTION OF PROMETHEUS' TORMENT IS BY FRENCH PAINTER GUSTAVE MOREAU.

ated with the tarot card called "The Lovers." The Koreans read here the story of a prince and his bride separated by her father-in-law, who was annoyed by the failed scheme of the prince to divert the "stars" of the Milky Way to water other stars. To escape the angry father, they can only meet if they cross the river. The Japanese story makes the spinning woman into the princess Shokujo, who is separated by a river from the shepherd, named Kinjin.

In ancient times, certain stars from this constellation were called Antinous, referring to the beautiful youth whom Hadrian loved. An Egyptian oracle warned Hadrian that either he or his beloved would die. Antinous threw himself into the Nile so that Hadrian could live, so strong was his love. An alternate version relates that Antinous drowned accidentally. Hadrian put his beloved's head on the coinage and named the city he built Antinoöpolis. A flower that sprouted from the blood of a lion that Hadrian killed (one thinks of Apollo's beloved, Hyacinthus, who was also immortalized in a flower) was also named after the tragic youth. Antinous was identified with Osiris, the Egyptian god beloved of Isis, and Dionysus, who, like Osiris, was dismembered and then reborn. The final tribute was to elevate Antinous to the stars.

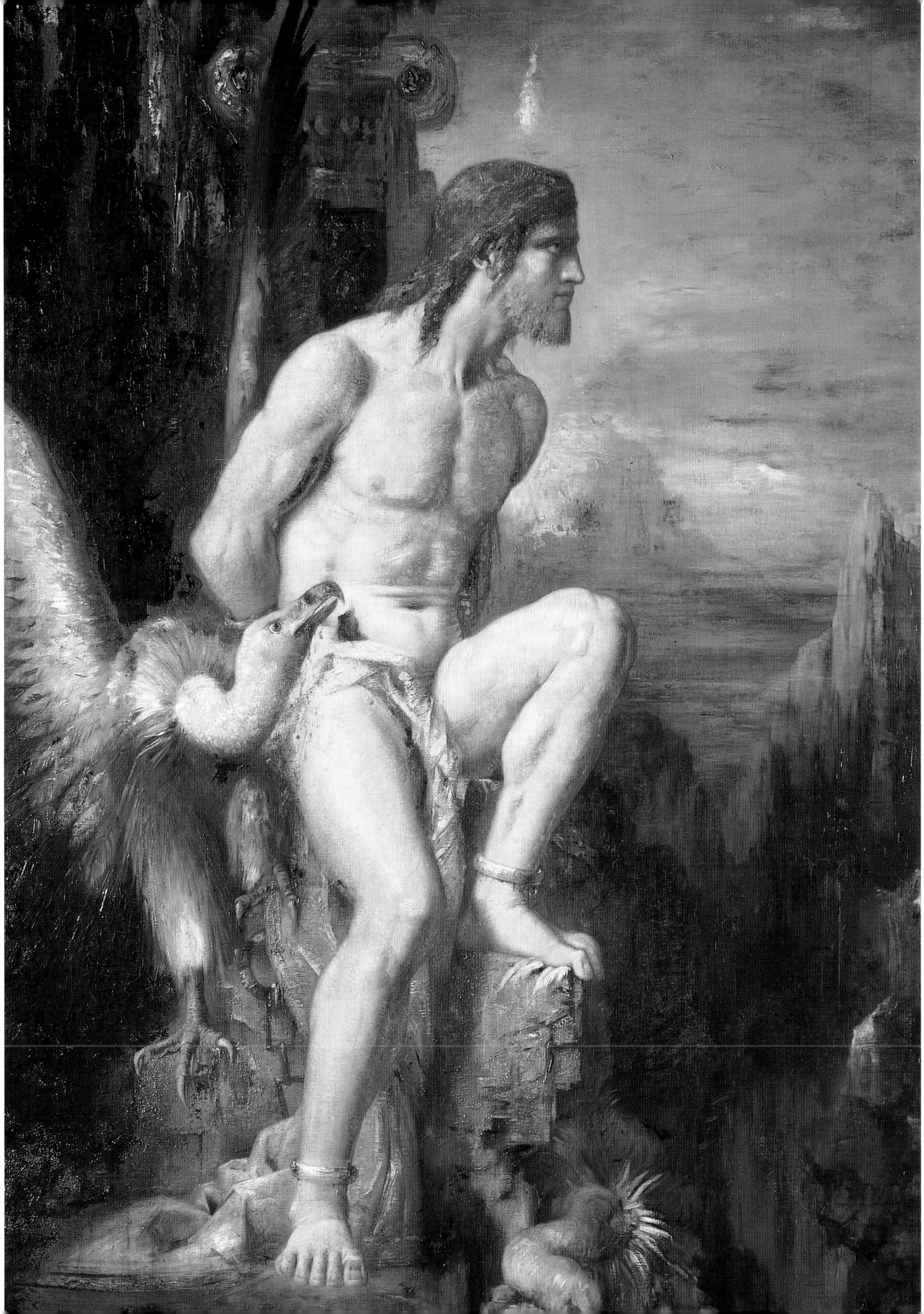

Aquila is also identified as the vulture that Zeus sent to punish Prometheus. One day. Prometheus asked Zeus to make a choice of two offerings: one was covered with rich fat (but concealed only bones), and the other was in a stomach and looked unappetizing (but held the delicious innards and rich flesh). Zeus took the pile wrapped in fat, and ever since receives that offering from votaries, whereas the mortals keep the edible parts for themselves. This trickery irritated Zeus, so the god took fire away from humankind (obviously shortsighted on his part, as fire was needed for sacrifice). Prometheus, as humankind's benefactor, did not want the mortals to suffer, so he stole some fire from the Olympians, hid it in a fennel stalk, and returned it to mankind. Zeus punished Prometheus by chaining him to a cliff and sending a vulture to tear Prometheus' liver apart each day; the immortal's liver grew back each night to be ready for the next day's excruciating torture.

Prometheus, the celebrated defender of mankind, who was abused by the tyrant Zeus, is the subject of a trilogy by Aeschylus. He is the personification of freedom, the individual who dares to make a free choice, regardless of the consequences. His name means "foresight," and he knew beforehand what he would suffer, yet still chose to do what he did. One can see why he is identified with Christ, who also sacrificed himself for love of man. The vulture was

This Laconian cup depicts Zeus and his eagle. Ever since its association with Zeus, the eagle has been used as a symbol of power. It was the imperial symbol of Rome; the Jews put it on the banners of the tribe of Dan; the double eagle

was the symbol of the Hapsburgs and also figured as a symbol of the Russian czars; stylized, the eagle was flown over the Third Reich; and in the United States the bald eagle represents the nation.

finally shot by Heracles when the hero freed Prometheus.

Some say that Aquila, Cygnus, and Vultur Cadens represent the Stymphalian birds killed by Heracles during his twelve labors. These horrible birds, like so many other of the monsters that Heracles slew, found their place in the heavens, immortalized as constellations.

In some cultures, the eagle is also a symbol of rebirth, just as the snake is a symbol of death. The eagle is a sign of the day, and the snake of the night. This symbolic opposition is beautifully illustrated by a Persian story that tells of an eagle that was freed by a prince from a snake that was strangling the bird. In return, the eagle brought seeds of the wine grape to the prince who had saved him, and so wine in Persia is traditionally considered the gift of the eagle.

The Babylonians tell a story about Etana, who flew on an eagle's back and was concealed in his feathers as he tried to take a plant sacred to Ishtar from heaven. This was a plant that relieves the pains of childbirth. He fell to the earth and was punished for his presumption (one sees a variation of the myths of both Bellerophon and Prometheus).

For the most part, the stories that surround the figure of the eagle are of regeneration and love. Only in the story of Prometheus do we see the eagle carrying out a cruel punishment. Thus, the eagle is a fertility symbol, a sign of life and the promise that it will be renewed.

'Αργώ

ARGO NAVIS

This constellation is in the portion of the sky associated with the sea. The most famous myth it represents is the story of Jason, sent to recover the golden fleece by the usurper Pelias, who had seized the throne of Iolcus from Jason's father, Pelias' half-brother, Aeson. Pelias wanted to kill Jason as much as Polydectes did Perseus. Jason set out on his quest in the Argo, which was named after its builder, Argos. It had fifty oars and as many heroes to ply them; Orpheus, the great musician of antiquity, played his lyre to inspire the heroes as they rowed. There was a piece in the prow from the sacred and prophetic wood of Dodona. There were many adventures

during the quest. For instance, in order to pass through the clashing rocks of the Symplegades on their way to Colchis, they released a dove and saw how it escaped with just its tail feathers clipped by the rocks. From the bird's example, they saw how to navigate the obstacle and made it through, although the colliding rocks destroyed a little piece of the stern. Apollonius Rhodius tells the full story of the *Argo*'s voyage in his *Argonautica* (third century B.C.). Euripides relates the sequel in his play *Medea* (431 B.C.). Charles Schneer made the film *Jason and the Argonauts*, which shows many of the hero's adventures. Jason was finally killed when a piece of *Argo*'s bow hit him on the head. Some say that the constellation has no bow; perhaps in this aspect it is faithful to the myth.

Other traditions say that this constellation commemorates the first ship ever to sail, perhaps the one that carried Danaus and his daughters from Egypt to Rhodes and then to Argos. Egyptians claim it carried Isis and Osiris over the sea when the world was flooded; the Hindus claimed the

48

same for their Isi and Iswara. The Arabs also named the constellation as a ship, *al Safinah*. Of course, it has been identified with Noah's Ark. In some parts of Africa this constellation was known as a horse.

One of the main stars in Argo Navis is Canopus, named after Menelaus' pilot, who brought Menelaus to Egypt, where the Spartan king regained his wife Helen (as Euripides tells us in his play *Helen*). In this version, Helen had not been kidnapped by Paris; instead, Zeus fashioned a figure out of a cloud, and this was the "Helen" that was kidnapped by Paris. The real Helen stayed safely in Egypt awaiting the return of her husband. Euripides tells us that Zeus decided on the Trojan War because the world was overpopulated (this was around 1200 B.C.; one wonders what Zeus would have thought

THIS RENAISSANCE PAINT-
ING BY COSTA LORENZO
DEPICTS A SCENE FROM
THE VOYAGE OF THE
ARGONAUTS.

about the world today). When the steadfast ship's pilot Canopus died, a city and a star were named after him as a tribute to his loyal service.

Argo Navis was called Agastya by the Hindus, after a sage who was the pilot of Argha. The Arabs called this star *Al Fahl*, "The Camel Stallion." We see again a link with a mode of transport, in this case "the ship of the desert." The brilliance of the star was said to lend fire to gems and give immunity from diseases. In Persia, *al-Anwar i Suhaili* meant the "Lights of Canopus" and referred to wise thought, the brilliance of the mind.

Canopus has also been called the Star of Osiris. It was used to announce the sunrise in autumn, and it was also associated with the god of waters. It is a favorable star, and promises renewal, as Osiris did. The Chinese called it *Laou Jin*, or "The Old Man." Christians called it the "Star of Saint Catherine" (a martyr who died around 307 A.D. in Alexandria)

We see not only heroes in the heavens but the things that helped them in their quests. A boat was important for people who fished and traded, so it was obvious that it would find its way into the heavens, as would a plow and wagon, so important for farmers.

βοώτης

BOÖTES

The name of this constellation probably comes from the Greek *Boos*, meaning "ox." Boötes was perceived as a driver of oxen, a herdsman (perhaps there is a relation to the French *bouvier*), or a hunter. Others relate this constellation to the bear, and one of its stars, Arcturus, may mean "the one who guards a bear" or it could refer to the bear's tail (*arctos* is "bear" in Greek). In the Roman comedian Plautus' play, *The Rope*, Arcturus delivers the prologue, saying, "I am a citizen of the heavenly city and the colleague of him who moves all the earth and the oceans....I shine brilliantly in the proper season both here and in the sky: I am called Arcturus. I and the other stars

pass to earth and spend time with mortals, and we make our reports...a word of advice, to you who are good, who lead lives properly, revering the gods and keeping the faith: keep on doing what you are doing, so that afterward you will be happy." Not only do we put our heroes among the stars, but the stars visit us to keep us in line.

Boötes is near Ursa Major, the Great Bear. The name of this constellation could also refer to one who drives a cart, since the star grouping sets late (the driver is considered one who drives slowly).

Boötes has also been associated with various people, including Lycaon, the father or grandfather of Callisto, whose story will be told under the constellation of the Great Bear. The constellation could also be Callisto's son Arcas. It has been seen as Horus, the Egyptian god. It has also been perceived by the Arabs as a shepherd who overlooks the flock of stars in the pasture around the North Pole. It also can be viewed as Osiris, whose dismemberment correlates with the setting of the constellation's various stars.

Another Greek who gave his name to this constellation was Iasion, the Titan whom Demeter met at the feast celebrating the wedding of Cadmus and Harmonia. They left the feast and went to mate in a ploughed field (Demeter's venue). They had two sons, Philomelus and Plutus. The wealthy Plutus did not share with Philomelus, who scraped and saved to buy oxen for the wagon that he invented. He plowed fields and made them fruitful, and for this earned his mother's approval. She placed him in the stars as Boötes. Plutus may be identified with Hades, the god of the underworld who kidnapped Kore, or Persephone, another child of Demeter, by Zeus, making Persephone Hades' cousin.

Atlas, the giant who holds up the world, is also a candidate for this particular constellation. He was condemned to holding up the world for being one of the Titans who had opposed Zeus in the latter's rise to power. One of Heracles' tasks was to get the apples of the Hesperides. Atlas knew where they were and had the

BELOW: IN THIS FIFTH-CENTURY B.C. GREEK MARBLE RELIEF, HERACLES (WITH A LITTLE HELP FROM HIS PROTECTOR ATHENA) HOLDS THE HEAVENS FOR ATLAS, WHO BRINGS THE STRONGMAN THE GOLDEN APPLES OF THE HESPERIDES. ALTHOUGH ATLAS IS IN ESSENCE A TRAGIC FIGURE WHO IS TAKEN ADVANTAGE OF, THIS LABOR IS PARTICULARLY GRATIFYING BECAUSE HERACLES SECURES HIS GOAL THROUGH WIT RATHER THAN FORCE.

OPPOSITE: CARAVAGGIO'S *THE YOUNG BACCHUS* DEPICTS DIONYSUS, GOD OF THE VINE, AT HIS MOST SANGUINE.

strength to get them, so Heracles offered to carry the universe while Atlas got the apples for him. When Atlas returned, he did not want to carry the heavens again. Heracles said he had an itch on his left shoulder and needed to scratch it. Atlas (who was not very bright) took the heavens back, but Heracles took the apples and did not even look back as he ran away. It is said that because Atlas was impolite to Perseus he was turned to stone for his rudeness and is now a gigantic mountain in North Africa. The Norse also had a legend about a quartet of dwarfs who support the sky at each corner of the world, representing the four directions.

Icarius, a peasant from an Athenian *deme* (to which he gave his name), has also given his name to this constellation. He introduced the grapevine in Greece when Pandion was king. His daughter Erigone was kind to Dionysus, and the god was taken by her charms. Some say she had a son named Staphylus (or "bunch of grapes") by Dionysus. Dionysus, gave her father a bottle of wine in a goatskin. (Other stories say a goat ate some of the vines and was killed for his *hybris*, eaten at a feast, and the goatskin used to make the first flask for carrying wine). Icarius served the wine to his neighboring shepherds, who thought he had poisoned them because the effects were so strange. They killed Icarius and left his body under a pine tree, but the dog Maera found it for Erigone. She hanged herself

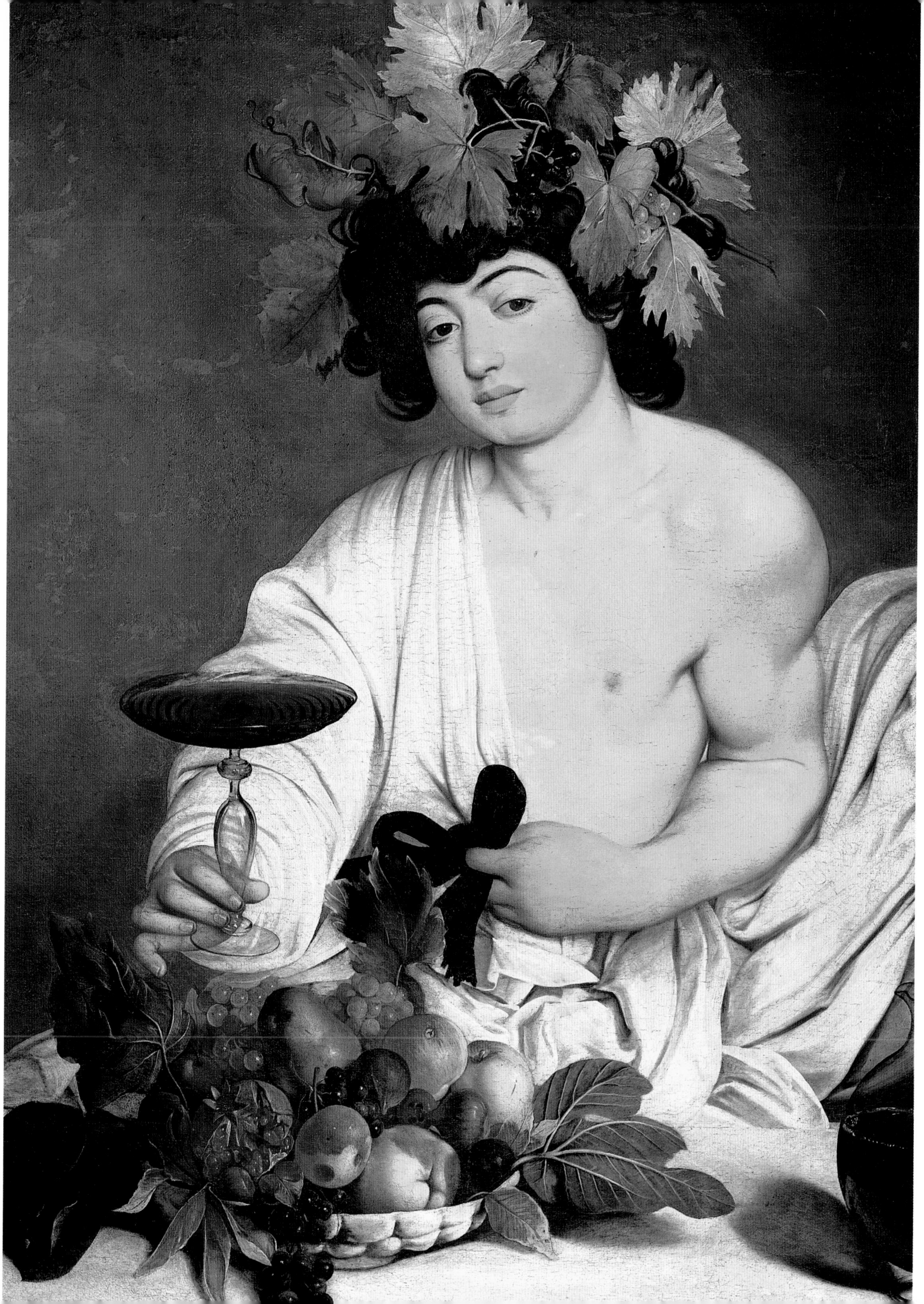

in sorrow, and the dog died shortly after in mourning for his mistress. In retribution, Dionysus cursed the maidens of Athens, who went mad and hanged themselves. The oracle at Delphi told the Athenians they had to have a festival to commemorate Erigone, during which the young girls would swing on trees to commemorate Icarius' loving daughter; this arc could represent the scythe that cut the grapes or it could relate to the dizziness associated with the consumption of wine.

Robert Graves sees the arc of the swing as symbolizing the rising and setting of the new moon; he also sees Maera as the name given to Hecuba after her transformation, and thus associated with the triple-headed goddess Hecate, the descendant of the original goddess who ruled Heaven, Earth, and Tartarus before being displaced by the patriarchal gods of ancient Greece. Hecuba is a potent fertility goddess. Later, masks replaced the girls on the swings, and this rite, called the *Aiora* (meaning "swing"), was said to lead to yearly fertility of the vine. The mythical associations are rich, describing the death that must precede birth or rebirth: the

ATHENIAN GIRLS SWING TO COMMEMORATE ERIGONE'S DEATH BY HANGING.

tearing apart of Dionysus and the crushing of the grape so that wine can be born.

The Greeks used the resin of pine to preserve their wine, and here we have the birth of retsina. Dionysus transformed Icarius into Boötes, Erigone into the constellation Virgo, and Maera into the star Procyon (the lesser dog star that rises before Sirius, the greater dog star), though there are some who identify Maera with Sirius.

The Arabs saw this constellation as a herdsman or a spear bearer, with Arcturus as the leg of the lance bearer. For the early Arabs, an enormous lion (*Asad*), covered this part of the heavens and Arcturus and Spica were part of it. Polish people see Boötes as forming part of the *Woz Niebeski*, "The Heavenly Cart." Christians called it Saint Sylvester; it was also thought to represent the prophet Amos.

Arcturus was regarded as baleful because of the associations of its rising and setting with storms. The Egyptians worshiped it. The Indians called it *Svati*, or "The Good Goer," or *Nishtya*, "Outcast." The Chinese called it *Ta Kio*, "The Great Horn," and the four stars near it *Kang Che*, or "Drought Lake." The Arabs called

it *al Haris al Sama*, or "The Keeper of Heaven and Hell," probably because it was visible so early in the evening—as if it were watching out for the other stars.

The Chinese saw one of the stars of this constellation as part of *Tseih Kung*, "The Seven Princes"; other of its stars as *Tso She Ti*, an offi-

THE CHINESE WERE APT TO PLACE GOVERNMENT OFFICIALS IN THE HEAVENS; THIS MAY REPRESENT *TSO SHE TI*, THE OFFICER WHO STANDS AT THE EMPEROR'S LEFT HAND.

cer in China who stands by the emperor's left hand; and still others *Yew She Ti*, an officer standing on the emperor's right hand.

This is an important constellation, associated with the wine and the grain, which in turn symbolize two necessary components of life: essence and quality.

΄Αρκτος

URSA MAJOR

This constellation involves Callisto ("most fair") and her son, Arcas, who was a candidate for the constellation Boötes. In some myths, Callisto is a wood nymph, in others she is the daughter of King Lycaon, and in still others the daughter of King Nycteus. She vowed to be a virgin, and kept the company of Artemis in the goddess' band of unwed maidens. Unfortunately, she caught Zeus' eye—always a disaster for the chaste—and he assumed the form of Artemis, or in some versions her brother Apollo, and in this form raped the virgin Callisto. She grew in size, showing the fruit of the union, which was noticed by Artemis one day when her band decided to bathe in a woodland pool. Artemis,

in anger, changed her into a bear (some said that Hera, Zeus' wife, did it out of jealousy, others that Zeus did it to save Callisto from Hera). Artemis then shot Callisto, but not before the young maiden gave birth to a son, Arcas (and, some add, the god Pan). Some say that Arcas hunted Callisto down. Zeus put her among the heavens as Ursa Major, or "The Great Bear." Others say that as Arcas was hunting her, Zeus transformed them both, Arcas into Arcturus, the "Guardian of the Bear." These constellations at the time of Homer never bathed in the ocean (that is, sank below the horizon), and Ovid tells us that Hera asked Poseidon never to let the slut Callisto and her bastard Arcas bathe in the ocean's waters.

Arcas gave his name to the Arcadians. It is said his grandfather Lycaon dismembered him and served him to Zeus, who immediately recognized the ruse, restored Arcas to life, and turned Lycaon into a wolf (his name is etymologically related to wolf).

Another Greek myth says that two bears protected Zeus and saved him from Cronus (Saturn), who would have killed him. For this, Zeus made them into Ursa Major (Helice) and Ursa Minor (Cynosura). A cynosure is something bright, distinguished, or notable—like a star—but the word literally means "tail of the dog."

This is the constellation that is probably the best known of all the stars, along with the three stars of Orion's belt. Most everyone in the West knows the Big Dipper, which forms the back and tail of Ursa Major. If one lines up the two stars of the dipper not connected to the handle and goes up from them, one can find the polestar, or Stella Polaris (so necessary for navigators), in Ursa Minor. The Norse call this star *Veraldar Nagli*, or "World Nail," because it keeps the heavens fixed. It is not really motionless, but it appears to be. The bear itself is obviously associated though northern climes, as Aristotle himself noted. The Phoenicians called this constellation *Kalitsah*, or "security."

The Big Dipper has been seen as the wheel of Ixion as it spins around the North Star (located in Ursa Minor). This constellation is also seen as a wagon, and Ixion may be related to the Sanskrit word for "axle," *áksa*. The Celtic King Arthur's name comes from *Arth*, or "Bear," and *Uthyr*, or "bright," "wonderful." Furthermore, this constellation, with its circular route, may have led to the notion of the round table. In Wales and England, Ursa Major is known as Arthur's Wain, or Wagon. In Ireland, it is King David's chariot, named after an early king. It is also a wain in Teutonic lore, and in France it took its place on coins as the "Great Chariot." It is also associated with

Charlemagne, and has been called Charles' Wain. The Poles called it *Woz Niebeski*, or "Heavenly Wain." In Egypt, this was dubbed the "Car of Osiris," although some saw it as a boat. In the works of Homer, these stars were called both a bear and a wagon, and Homer also noted that these stars do not dip into the ocean.

These northern stars have also been called the plow, pulled by Seven Oxen (*Septem Triones,* which became *septentrion*, or "north," as *arctos*, "bear," led to the word "Arctic"). Other etymologies suggest simply "Seven Stars." Similar appellations are found in England and India. There have been many different interpretations of this constellation, and particularly its famous seven stars. Hunters saw a bear, farmers a plow, sailors a ship, and merchants a wagon. The French saw it as a casserole, a knife, or a brooding hen followed by her chicks— the associations with food are obvious. The Skidi Pawnees saw it as a stretcher with a sick man on it. Some Siberians called these stars the seven watchmen, who guarded the North Pole. Others in Siberia saw them as seven Khans, or seven brothers, seven blacksmiths, seven skulls, or simply seven old men. Ancient Mayans saw these famous seven stars as a mythological parrot called "Seven Macaw."

The Chinese, as usual, saw the stars as the obedient court or government, with the North Star as the emperor. The farmers, however, saw it as *Pih Tow*, "The Bushel," and mystics saw it as *Tien Li*, "Heavenly Reason." The Hebrews, also farmers, saw a woman sifting grain. The Chinese have also called it *Ti Tche*, or "The Emperor's Chariot," a designation that no doubt indicated communication with the West. Christians who fished saw it as Saint Peter's Boat.

There is a story in Germany that says the Big Dipper is the *Himmelwagen*, or "Heavenly Cart." They speak of Hans Dumkin, who, although he was poor, offered his hospitality to Christ. He had always wanted to travel, so Christ gave him his own cart (the dipper), and he became the star Alcor, enabling him to continue sightseeing for eternity. This recalls the story of Hyrieus entertaining the gods (although he did not know who his guests were) and being rewarded with the son he had longed for, Orion.

The Arabs saw the dipper as a funeral procession, with the stars of the dipper as the coffin and the handle as mourners. Christians saw it as the litter of Lazarus and the mourners Mary, Martha, and Mary Magdalene.

North American Indians, such as the Housatonics and the Canadian Micmac Indians, had a story associated with the stars of this constellation and those of Boötes and Corona Borealis. They saw the Corona Borealis as the bear's den, the cup of the dipper as the bear, and the stars as the various bear hunters, named for the birds that the colors and sizes of the stars suggested: robin, chickadee, cowbird, pigeon, blue jay, and two owls. The star Alcor was the pan in which one of the hunters would cook the meat. The myth goes something like this: the chickadee calls the other hunters when the bear comes out in the spring. The hunters set out in a pursuit that lasts all summer. One by one, they give up (beginning in October, some of these stars are no longer visible), but finally the remaining hunters catch the bear. The robin hits the bear and topples her (the bear is on its back in relation to Polaris in winter). The robin is covered with blood that he shakes off, except for a bit on his

breast. This blood falls on some maple trees, and the leaves turn red. The chickadee and the others cut up the meat and cook it. The winter sky sees the skeleton of the bear, but another bear will be born, hibernating. In the spring, the hunt begins again. Interestingly, the Algonquins and the Narragansetts called the North Star "The Bear."

In the *Kalevala* (the Finnish national epic, published in 1835 by Löhnrot, who painstakingly compiled the accompanying songs as well) this constellation is called Otava and Otavainen, which may indicate the king of the beasts. The Danes call it *Karlsvogn* and the Swedes *Karlavagn*; *Karl* is associated with the god Odin (or Wotan or Woden) and means, roughly, "Mr. Big." In Iceland it is *Stóri Vagn,* "Great Wagon," or *Stóri Björn,* "Great Bear." Saxons called it *Irmines Wagen.*

The seven main stars have various designations, as we have seen, including the seven wise men of Greece. In India, it was seen as *Saptar Shayar,* or "The Seven Anchorites." One star was seen as Vashishtha, one of the seven sages. The Sanskrit name *Riksha* can mean either "bear" or "star."

One wonders about the communication among the many cultures that saw similar interpretations of this constellation, a guide to so many ships. The seven stars that revolve around the North Star lead to obvious associations with a vehicle that moves, but that so many peoples—from the Mediterranean to North America—saw the figure as a bear is indeed astonishing.

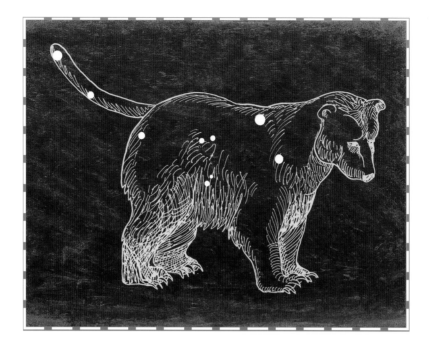

Κυνόσουρα

URSA MINOR

This is the constellation that is closest to the North Pole and, like Ursa Major, it circles the polestar. Its name means "The Lesser Bear." Tradition has it that that this constellation was created in part by clipping Draco's (the dragon's) wings. Now Draco appears as a wingless snake.

The name the Phoenicians gave to this constellation was *Cynosura*, or the "Tail of the Dog." The Gaels also named these stars after a tail, namely *Drag-Blod*, or "The Fire Tail." The Egyptians saw it as the Dog of Set, and it was associated with

OPPOSITE: A COMPANION OF ARTEMIS, CALLISTO WAS SEDUCED BY ZEUS. ENRAGED, ARTEMIS TRANSFORMED THE MAIDEN INTO A BEAR. CALLISTO WAS SAVED FROM THE HUNT BY ZEUS, WHO PLACED HER IMAGE IN THE STARS. THE AFFAIR IS CELEBRATED IN JEAN HONORÉ FRAGONARD'S *JUPITER ET CALLISTO*.

drought and the dreaded jackal. We have mentioned that this constellation has been associated with Arcas, the son of Callisto, and with one of the two Cretan bears that took good care of Zeus on Mount Ida when he needed it. It is also possible that this is a dog that has been linked with Callisto.

The Arabs called this constellation *Al Dubb al Asghar*, or "The Lesser Bear." They also saw it as a fish, and in the more essential application of "the hole in which the earth's axle fitted." The Persians saw the stars as date-palm seeds, or fruit. This

60

may be the Babylonian leopard, a figure that circled the pole. In the West, this constellation is known as the "Little Dipper."

The Danes, Swedes, Icelanders, and Finns called it the "Smaller Chariot," "Throne of Thor," or sometimes "Odin." Some say its stars are "Milkmaids of the Sky."

Spanish shepherds called this *Bocina*, or "bugle." Italian sailors saw a snake, *Bogina*, or the

THIS ROMANTICIZED ENGRAVING SHOWS THE PROPHET ELIJAH AS HE RIDES IN A CHARIOT TOWARD HEAVEN. THIS HEBREW PROPHET UPHELD THE WORSHIP OF YAHWEH OVER THE PHOENICIAN GOD BAAL.

boa. Christians identify it with the chariot that Joseph sent to his father, or then again as the chariot that transported Elijah to heaven. In addition, it may represent the bear that the Christian hero David killed.

The star Polaris, or the polestar, is a useful guide for sailors. The Chinese may have called it *How Kung*, "The Empress," but the most common name for the polestar is *Tien Hwang Ta Ti*: "The Great

61

Imperial Ruler of Heaven." The circling stars worship it and are its subjects, or, in some cases, the stars represent the "Emperor's Seat." *Stella Polaris* became *Stella Maris*, and the latter was also a title of the Virgin Mary; the *Maris* portion may be a reference to Miriam, her name in Hebrew, rather than to the sea.

The Finns called this star *Taehti*, or "The Star at the Top of the Heavenly Mountain." It was a steering star, or the lodestar, for early English sailors. Milton in his *Comus* called it "Our Star of Arcady, /Or Tyrian Cynosure," and Helena in Shakespeare's *A Midsummer Night's Dream* compliments Hermia's eyes: "Your eyes are lodestars." Shakespeare also uses it to characterize Caesar in *Julius Caesar*:

> *If I could pray to move, prayers would move me;*
> *But I am constant as the Northern Star,*

THIS DRAMATIC DETAIL OF A WALL PAINTING BY CORREGGIO DEPICTS THE CORONATION OF MARY, QUEEN OF HEAVEN, WITH A TIARA OF STARS.

> *Of whose true-fixed and resting quality*
> *There is no fellow in the firmament.*
> *The skies are painted with unnumbered sparks,*
> *They are all fire, and every one doth shine,*
> *But there's but one in all doth hold his place.*

In India, this star was *Grahadhara*, or "Pivot of the Planets," sometimes identified with the god Dhruva. It helped the Arabs orient themselves toward Mecca, the place Muslims must face during worship. The Turks called it *Yilduz*, or simply "The Star"; its light was said to disappear for a while after the Turks captured Constantinople (one wonders if this is a Christian myth in which the stars lamented the loss of their sacred city).

This reliable star has shed its light on the dreams of men and women throughout the ages. It is a trusty fixture in the sky and is widely worshiped.

Ἡρακλῆς

HERACLES

The hero of this constellation, Heracles to the Greeks, has already figured in some of the aforementioned accounts. He is depicted as a kneeling figure, holding a club. He held the heavens for Atlas, represented by Boötes, when he went to find the golden apples of the Hesperides. Since he will figure in several other constellations, it is worth relating some of the stories of this famous hero.

Heracles is a touchstone for myths. He is probably the greatest hero of Greece. He rid the land of monsters and made it fit for civilization. But he shared some of the char-acteristics of the monsters he defeated. He was notorious for his excessive appetites, whether for food or sex. It was the latter that proved his downfall. He brought his latest love—a princess for whose sake he had sacked a city—home to his wife. In order to regain his love, his wife sent him a charm entrusted to her by a dying centaur, Nessus, whom Heracles had dealt a mortal blow. This charm was a cloak soaked in the dying centaur's blood, which turned out to be a poison that ate into the skin; also, the cloak was impossible to remove. Heracles begged to be immolated on a pyre to escape the

torture. As Sophocles' Lichas says in *Trachinians*, "Heracles defeated all, but was himself defeated by love." The cloak that burned him with its consuming flames was like the passion that consumed him from within.

Heracles was the son of Zeus and Alcmena, who was married to Amphitryon. Zeus made love to her by assuming the shape of her husband while he was away on a military expedition. Heracles' name means "Glory of Hera," because he did so many tasks in her name to earn purification. Both his grandfathers are sons of Perseus and Andromeda.

There are twelve major labors with which Heracles is associated. One account says that he was enslaved to his cousin Eurystheus to atone for his crimes—most likely for killing his children, which he did when he suffered from a madness visited upon him by Hera. He also killed Iphitus, for which crime he was a slave to the queen Omphale for three years. He killed his tutor Linus in response to a rebuke. Clearly, Heracles was one to be reckoned with. His lustful energy is illustrated by his adventures at the court of Thespius, the king of a country near Thebes. Heracles hunted a lion that was plaguing Cithaeron, and after fifty days he found it and killed it. Thespius wanted grandchildren from Heracles, and he had fifty daughters. Each night that Heracles returned exhausted from hunting, a new daughter was waiting for him. He thought she was the same one

THIS SEVENTEENTH-CENTURY PAINTING BY GUIDO RENI DEPICTS HERACLES' WIFE, DEIANEIRA, BEING CARRIED OFF BY THE CENTAUR NESSUS, WHO WAS SUBSEQUENTLY SLAIN BY HERACLES. BEFORE HE DIED, HOWEVER, THE CENTAUR GAVE DEIANEIRA A GIFT THAT WOULD PROVE DEADLY FOR HER HUSBAND: A LOVE CHARM THAT LED TO HIS APOTHEOSIS, JUST AS LOVE HAD TEMPERED HIS MONSTROUS NATURE.

because it was always dark and he was always tired. The result was fifty sons, called the Thespiades.

The twelve labors may be regarded allegorically as tasks to be accomplished for the purification of the soul or perhaps as a commemoration of the twelve seasons, with Heracles as a type of sun god accomplishing his labors as the sun goes through its yearly cycle. Heracles became a great Stoic hero, and was celebrated as such in Seneca's tragedies. The first six of the labors were performed in the Peloponnesus of southern Greece. The other six took place all over, including the underworld; the three final labors were metaphors for death and the search for immortality.

The first labor was to kill the Nemean lion, a brother of the sphinx (part woman, part lion, and winged), the monster that Oedipus slew after solving its riddle: "What goes on four feet in the morning, two at noon, and three in the evening?" (The answer was "man.") This lion was killing everything it saw in the region of Nemea, and it was invulnerable to weapons. Heracles strangled it, and then wore its skin and used its head as a helmet. There is another version saying that Heracles had to kill it by using its own claws on itself. It is said that this is the lion that is the constellation Leo, a tribute to Heracles' prowess.

The destruction of the Lernaean Hydra was the second labor. The Hydra was a snakelike creature haunting the marsh of Lerna, from which it emerged to ravage the countryside. It had possibly a hundred—but in most accounts nine—heads that would grow again if cut off—and one head was immortal. The Hydra was a favorite of Hera, and she sent a giant crab, or crayfish, to help it in the fight against Heracles, but the hero was able to stomp on the crustacean and incapacitate it. Heracles, on the advice of Athena, asked his nephew Iolaus to cauterize each neck as Heracles cut the heads off, in this way preventing them from growing again. Heracles buried the immortal head and covered it with a big stone, which can be found to this day on the road from Lerna to Elaeus. Hera put the crab in the constellations as the constellation Cancer to reward it for faithful service.

Next came the slaughter of the Erymanthian boar, which was laying Mount Erymanthus to waste. Heracles kept it running until it fell from exhaustion, enabling the hero to deliver the fatal blow. The hind of Ceryneia was the next monster Heracles had to destroy; not only was the creature vicious, but it bore golden horns that were formidable weapons. It was sacred to Artemis. Some accounts say that Heracles killed the hind after wounding it as it was crossing a river in Arcadia. Others accounts state that Heracles merely captured the beast.

The Stymphalian birds were eating all the fruit of Arcadia, after which they would hide. Athena helped Heracles to flush them out, giving him some bronze castanets with which to frighten the birds. As the birds flew out of their lair, Heracles was able to shoot them. Some say that these birds had metal feathers, which they fired at their victims.

THIS ROMAN STATUE SHOWS HERACLES, WITH HIS CLUB AND LION SKIN, HOLDING ONE OF HIS SONS.

Augeas, the king of Elis, kept herds given him by his father Helios, and his stables were a complete mess. The dung had accumulated for years, and the surrounding fields were barren because they lacked fertilizer. Heracles was told by Augeas that if he completed the task of cleaning the stables in one day he would be given part of his kingdom. This inspired Heracles, who diverted two streams, Alpheus and Peneus, so that they coursed through the stables, quickly cleaning up the mess (a Herculean task indeed).

The labors then left the Peloponnese. The Cretan bull may have been the same one that abducted Europa for Zeus, or it may be the bull that Minos, the king of Crete (Pasiphae's husband), was told to sacrifice to Zeus, but did not because of its beauty. Some accounts say that Zeus made Pasiphae fall in love with the animal and that she subsequently engaged the services of Daedalus to build her a hollow frame in the form of a heifer that allowed her to mate with it. Pasiphae then gave birth to the minotaur, half-bull and half-man. Its home was the labyrinth and it was fed boys and girls from Athens until Theseus killed it (but that is another story). Heracles was given permission from Minos to catch the Cretan bull, which he did, swimming across the sea to deliver it to Eurystheus. It is said that the animal escaped and ravaged the Peloponnesus until Theseus overcame it near Marathon. Thus was the seventh labor completed.

Diomedes, the king of Thrace, had four mares that were wild and vicious, feeding on human flesh. One legend has it that Heracles gave the mares their master Diomedes to eat, after which the steeds allowed themselves to be led away, tamed at last. Heracles was also sent to obtain the belt of Hippolyta, queen of the Amazons. One story says that Hippolyta was killed in a fight, another that she handed the belt over to regain her companion Melanippe, who had been seized. In any case, Heracles succeeded in his ninth labor.

The next three tasks have to do with the underworld, the afterlife, and the Great Unknown (which is to say the uncharted regions of the West, beyond the edge of the ocean). Geryon, the son of Chrysaor (the brother of Medusa), had a large herd of cattle guarded by a ferocious two-headed dog, Orthrus. The island where the herd grazed was in the West (that is, at the earth's extreme edge). Heracles had to borrow the cup of the sun (using physical coercion on the sun itself to gain his request) to cross the ocean to sail to the West. Heracles also had to bully the ocean to still its waves. With relative ease, Heracles killed Orthrus, the guard Eurytion, and Geryon with his huge club. On the way home, Heracles erected the Pillars of Heracles (which are known today as the Rock of Gibraltar and the Rock of Ceuta) to commemorate his adventures in this region.

Heracles also sacked the underworld, in order to bring back Cerberus, the great three-headed guard dog. While there, Heracles freed Theseus, who had been chained in the underworld for trying to kidnap Persephone. Hades gave Heracles permission to borrow the fearsome dog—provid-

ABOVE: THIS DETAIL FROM A MARBLE SARCOPHAGUS DEPICTS A FEW OF HERCULES' TWELVE LABORS.

ed the hero could subdue the animal without weapons. Heracles did this with his bare hands, although he was stung many times by the dog's two forked tongues, which contained venom. Eurystheus was so frightened when he saw the dog that he hid in a jar. Heracles returned Cerberus to Hades, having completed this arduous task.

The final task was the acquisition of the golden apples of the Hesperides (the Hesperides were nymphs of the evening), which had been given to Hera by Gaia as a wedding gift. The apples were so precious that a dragon with a hundred heads, Ladon (the son of Phorcys and Ceto, according to some accounts, Typhon and Echidna according to others, and Gaia in yet others), was set to guard them. On his way to get the apples, Heracles freed Prometheus from the terrible punishment that Zeus had inflicted on him for bringing fire to man (see Aquila). After Heracles slew the dragon and had the apples in his possession (thanks to Atlas), the Hesperides were transformed into the elm, poplar, and willow (in which form they weep for eternity for the loss of the apples). The dragon was immortalized as Draco, a constellation commemorating Heracles' victory and the dragon's faithful service to Hera.

The apples were eventually returned to the garden, their proper home. Symbolically, these gleaming golden apples can be identified with the bright setting sun—appropriately, they are found in the West. They could also represent

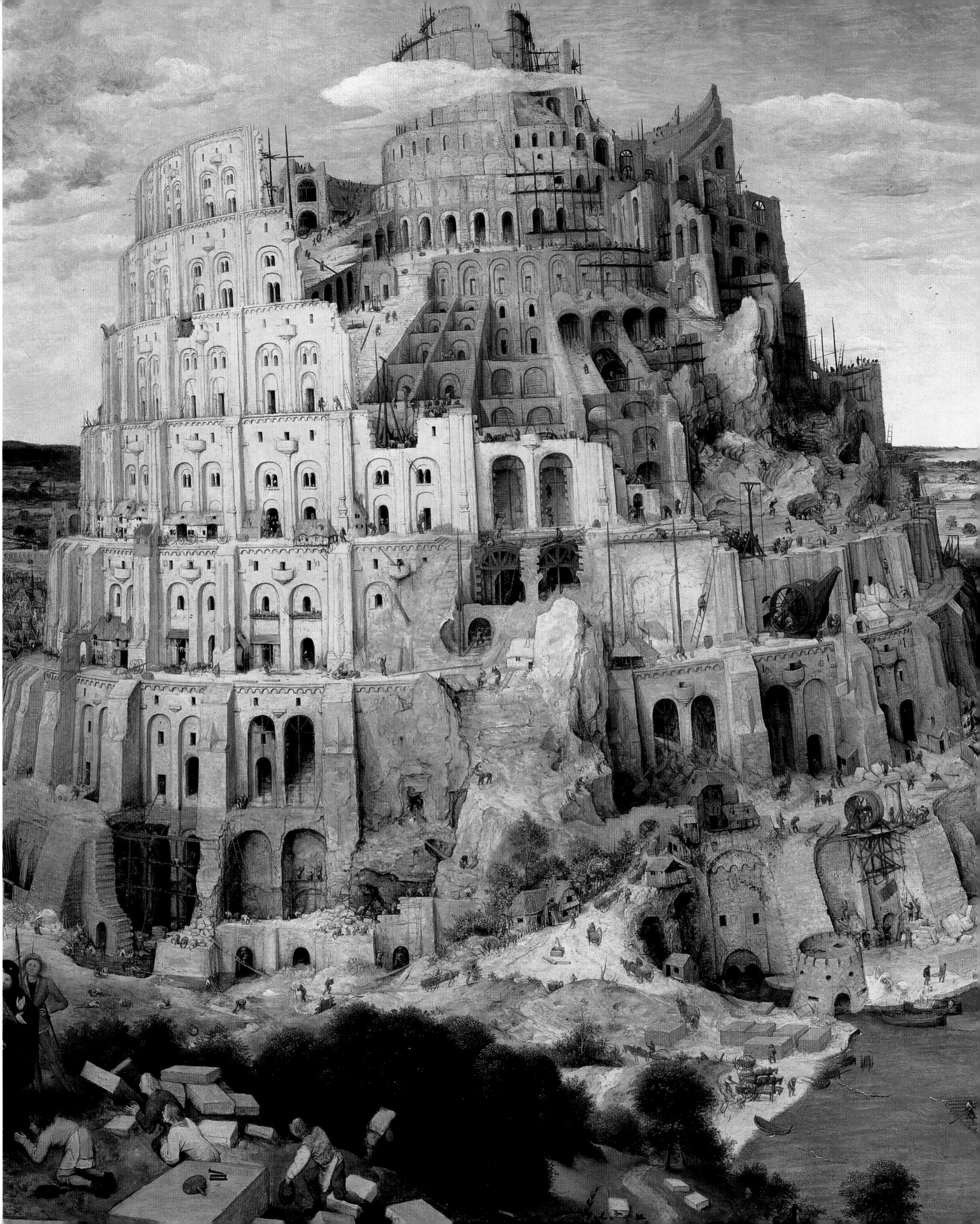

the stars that come out in the evening (note that Hesperus is the evening star sacred to Aphrodite). The golden apples can be identified with life (which as we know it requires the sun to thrive); it is easy to extend the image—considering that the apples are a source of nourishment—so that the apples of the Hesperides symbolize immortal life. This recalls both ambrosia, the food of immortality eaten by the gods in Greek myth, and the apples of eternal youth in Teutonic lore, the food of the gods tended by Freya; this tale is recounted in Wagner's *Das Rheingold*.

Heracles had many other adventures before he died. But he was awarded with immortality and given Hera's daughter Hebe, the goddess of youth, as his immortal wife. A local boy from Argos who made good through his own efforts in spite of enormous odds against him, Heracles was more than a superman, because he was a mortal man who struggled valiantly and never gave up.

The constellation of Hercules/Heracles is appropriately near the constellation Draco, which has also been associated with Tiamat and the Lernaean Hydra. Thus, Heracles is identified with Marduk, the Assyrian god who was victorious over the dragon Tiamat, slicing her in half and thereby creating the earth and heavens. Her blood became the rich oil of the lands. The constellations in the sky were formed from the

OPPOSITE: THIS PAINTING BY SIXTEENTH-CENTURY FLEMISH MASTER PIETER BREUGHEL THE ELDER DEPICTS THE TOWER OF BABEL. THE EPISODE SUGGESTS THAT THE PROLIFERATION OF CULTURE AND LANGUAGE IN THE WORLD WAS GOD'S PUNISHMENT FOR MAN'S PRIDE, BUT THE REMARKABLE INSIGHTS THAT ARE REVEALED THROUGH A COMPARATIVE STUDY OF WORLD CULTURES SUGGESTS THAT SUCH DIVERSITY IS A BLESSING.

ABOVE: SEVENTEENTH-CENTURY FLEMISH MASTERS PETER PAUL RUBENS AND JAN BREUGHEL COLLABORATED ON THIS ILLUSTRATION OF ADAM AND EVE IN THE GARDEN OF EDEN.

bodies of her allies in the fight. Human beings was formed from the blood and bones of the giant Qingu, another of her allies, and a bit of clay. Human beings were created to serve the gods. The ziggurats, or sacred towers (also observatories)—one of which was the Tower of Babel—were dedicated to Bel-Marduk.

The Phoenicians called this constellation Melkarth, after their sea god (remember that Heracles mastered the ocean on his way to the garden of the Hesperides). One biblical association is with Adam (perhaps from the relationship with the apple), another with Samson, the strongman. The Christians saw the constellation as the Three Magi.

The Arabs saw various things in the sky at this region, from a pasture to a row of pearls. What was construed as the club of Hercules was called by the Arabs "Sheep within the Pasture." The Chinese saw it as "The Emperor's Seat," which is significant since Chinese emperors were traditionally associated with the sun. Some other stars were called "In the River" (or "Between the River"), and others "Heaven's Record," "The Nine Rivers," and "The Middle Mountain." Some even located the Apex of the Sun's Way in this constellation, a tribute to Heracles as a sun-related god, who toiled his way through life as the sun toils its way through the year, day by day heroically overcoming night to shine forth in victory.

69

DRACO

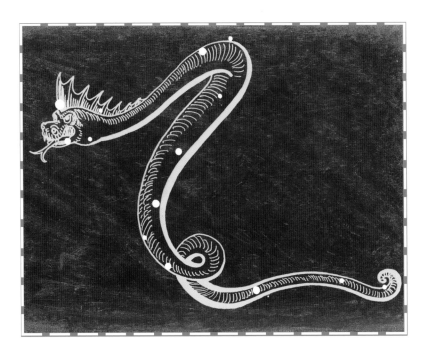

As has been mentioned, this constellation is associated with the dragon Ladon from the tale of the golden apples of the Hesperides (see Heracles and Boötes). In antiquity, the polestar was not Polaris but Thuban, located in Draco. One of the stars in this constellation is called the Zenith star, and it circles the pole. Long ago, this important star was the closest star to the pole.

The Sumerians called Thuban *Tiranna,* or "Light of Paradise." Enlil, the god of the sky who created the earth and humans and all the heav-

ens, is associated with this star. The Egyptians oriented pyramids, such as those at Abousseir and Giza, toward this star; in fact, the pyramid of Cheops was designed so that Thuban shone through one of its passages each night.

The snake has long been a prominent symbol in many different cultures; for example, to some peoples, the snake represented fertility and life, and to others death. Its venom is potentially fatal and yet is used to create healing medicine. The snake was also a symbol of renewal, or resurrection, because the serpent renews itself by shedding its skin.

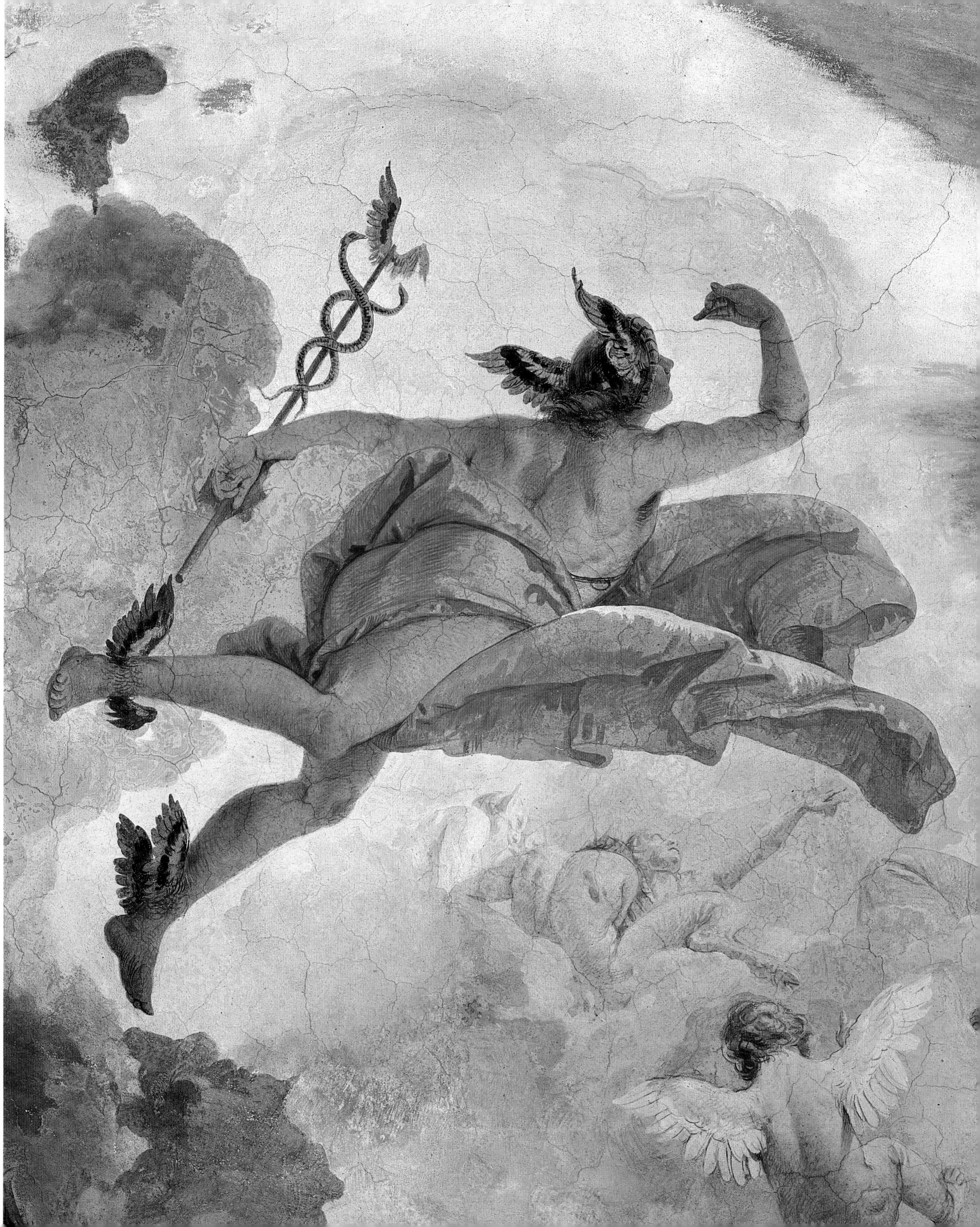

Among many cultures, there was a myth describing a snake encircling the globe; to the Greeks, it was the *ourobouros*, a giant snake that eats its tail. In Orphic lore, a snake circles an egg (perhaps representing death as a limit of life). The caduceus, the staff used by Hermes to guide souls to the underworld, depicts, two snakes entwined (a motif used by doctors, which was introduced by Hippocrates to symbolize the capacity for healing). In Japan, blood from a poisonous pit viper *(mamushi)* is drunk to increase sexual potency.

Snakes were sacred in the Roman household because they were thought to represent the souls of the dead. These domestic reptiles were served food because the fortune of the house was thought to depend on their happiness. Joseph Campbell speaks of the two snakes in Indian lore represented as intertwining in the human system, around the *chakras*, as symbols of life. This could relate to the divine couple in the Chinese pantheon who put the universe in order: Nü Kua and Fu Xi. Their top halves were human, but their bottom halves were intertwined snakes. They were male and female, or yin and yang. They established the directions of the compas and made sure that world order was maintained, with everything interacting properly.

The snake was the disguise taken by the devil in the Garden of Eden to seduce Eve (who in turn seduced Adam) into committing the first sin (by eating the forbidden apple of knowledge). It is noteworthy that the source of evil

OPPOSITE: THIS MAGNIFICENT DETAIL ILLUSTRATES MERCURY (HERMES) AS HE FLIES ACROSS THE HEAVENS CARRYING HIS CADUCEUS, THE SNAKE-ENTWINED STAFF THAT EVEN TODAY IS A SYMBOL OF THE MEDICAL PROFESSION.

ABOVE: THIS *LARARIUM* SHOWING SEVERAL PEOPLE AND A SNAKE WAS TAKEN FROM THE RUINS OF POMPEII. *LARES* WERE TUTELARY SPIRITS ASSOCIATED WITH THE GODDESS VESTA AND WERE GUARDIANS— ALONG WITH SNAKES—OF THE ROMAN HOUSEHOLD.

in both Greek mythology and biblical lore—the most influential canons in Western culture—are women: Pandora and Eve.

The snake is also often identified with evil, probably because it was such a powerful symbol in some of the religions that were in competition with Judaism and Christianity. And, since the best way to defeat old gods is to demonize them, many cultures, did just that.

The Greeks demonized the mother goddesses of earlier cultures, and early Christians demonized the snake. Apollo, the rational sun god, defeated a goddess and her representative, the serpent Python, when he took over Delphi. Likewise, the Greek *daimon* and its mainly benevolent services were transformed by Christian culture into something more sinister, as is shown in the word *demon*. Interestingly, another Christian association is with the Holy Innocents of Bethlehem.

As already mentioned, Draco is associated with the Sumerian dragon Tiamat. Tiamat was split in two, and one half became Draco and the other Hydra. Arabic nomads saw the stars that form the head of Draco as "Five Camels Trotting Along in the Desert." Some Arabs called these stars "Lute Player" and "Dancer." Egyptians associated the constellation Draco with Isis. In Persia, this constellation was *Azhdeha*, or a "man-eating serpent"; according to the Hindus, these stars represented an alligator. The dragon is the national symbol of China, but the Chinese call Draco

73

Tsi Kung, "The Palace of the Heavenly Emperor" (the Chinese locate their dragon in the constellation known to the West as Libra). The Hebrews saw Draco as a quiver. A Swedish account states that this constellation represents the Baltic Sea.

Serpentine creatures are plentiful in Greek mythology. Indeed, Draco's name comes from the Greek *derkein*, which means "to see" (a snake's eyes never seem to close, making it a guard par excellence). The word *dragon* comes from the same root. Appropriately, this constellation never sets. It was once winged, but Thales used the wings when he outlined the shape of the constellation Ursa Minor. Draco also represents the dragon watching the Golden Fleece, which Medea overcame with magic herbs. Draco may also represent Ladon, the dragon slain by Heracles, or it may simply represent the dragon depicted on the Shield of Heracles. Draco may also be the snake that Athena seized from the giants and threw up to the sky. It could be the dragon killed by Cadmus when he founded Thebes, from whose sown teeth sprang both fighting men and civilians to populate his city (the population of which was known as "dragon-born"). The list is vast.

THIS NINETEENTH-CENTURY PAINTING BY GUSTAVE MOREAU ILLUSTRATES THE EARLY, POSITIVE RELATIONSHIP BETWEEN JASON AND MEDEA. SHE IS ASSOCIATED WITH DRACO BECAUSE THE SNAKE SYMBOLIZED HER MAGICAL POWERS.

This powerful constellation located near Cygnus, the swan, is representative of the earth, as the swan is of the heavens. Depicted with wings, the dragon is a potent symbol of fertility (we have mentioned already the winged phalloi depicted in antiquity). In Seneca's tragedy *Medea* (based on Euripides' play of the same name), Medea harnesses the powers of the universe to aid her in punishing her errant lover, Jason. Stating that the snakes of earth are not sufficient agents of her wrath, she draws on heaven, invoking the constellation Draco: she asks Ophiuchus to relax his hold on the snake he carries and let the poisons flow forth. She also calls on Python, Hydra, and the dragon that guarded the Golden Fleece. The snake, initially symbolic of fertility, as Medea's love for Jason was fertile in the beginning, has come to represent destruction, as illustrated by Medea's revenge against Jason.

Draco and its myths touch some of the fundamental drives of human beings—the search for fertility, the fear of death, and so on. It shines as an embodiment of the complexity of human interaction.

H Y D R A

Many of the symbolic resonances regarding Draco also apply to Hydra, the multiheaded monster slain by Heracles (for instance, the Greeks also associated this constellation with the dragon that guarded the Golden Fleece). The Hydra was a water monster. Some say that Draco breathed fire; in contrast, the Hydra has a name that derives from the Greek word for "water" and was a slimy moist creature that lived happily in the Lernean swamp. This constellation is located in the area of the sky that was called the sea.

In Indian lore, this constellation was identified with Vritra, the monster that the sun god Indra had to over-come. In the winter solstice, the stars of Hydra shine brightly throughout the night, as if to challenge the sun, which is at its least powerful at this time. It is said that the time of the summer solstice commemorates the sun's (and Indra's) victory; accordingly, Hydra becomes invisible at this time of the year. As noted above, Aquila brought Indra the mystical drink associated with the moon, called soma, to revive his spirits during his great contest with the forces of darkness; thus, the rainy season began with the triumph of Indra.

In Sumerian lore, Hydra is identified with half of the vanquished dragon Tiamat. The battle in which Tiamat fell is commemorated every year at the time of the summer solstice, reaffirming the supremacy of Marduk over the forces of darkness and chaos.

The Chinese call one of the Sieu (lunar nodes, or loci of stars, usually associated with twenty-eight famous generals) in this constellation "Willow Wreath." The home of the planet Saturn and a symbol for immortality, this constellation was said to rule the planets; it was worshiped dur-ing the summer solstice. One star was called the "House of the Sun" and another the "House of the Moon."

The Arabs call one star of Hydra *al-Fard al-Shuja*, "The Solitary One of the Serpent," demonstrating that the Greek and the Arabic cultures probably communicated early on in their cultural histories.

Now that we have reviewed the major stars associated with Heracles (whose name will appear again), we return to the alphabetical list.

THIS FIFTEENTH-CENTURY ITALIAN MEDALLION DEPICTS THE BATTLE BETWEEN HERACLES AND THE HYDRA.

CANIS MAJOR

The dog has been man's best friend for millennia. Argos, the faithful dog of Ulysses, waited for years for his master to return (twenty, in fact: ten while he was away at war in Troy and ten during which he wandered, as recounted in Homer's *Odyssey*). When Argos recognized his master upon the latter's return (as many of the humans did not), the canine died from happiness. A common name for a dog is "Fido," from the Latin *fidus*, meaning "faithful."

The most famous star in Canis Major is Sirius, the dog star. Arguably the brightest star in the heavens, it rises at dawn during the summer solstice. The Egyptians likened this star to Anubis, the dog-headed god, considered the watchdog of the

seasons. The rising of this star was important for calculating the flooding of the Nile, and marked the beginning of the new year. Temples of Isis were oriented toward this star (whereas Osiris' temples are oriented toward Orion). The Egyptians also interpreted this star as of a cow with a disc and horns, called Isis Hathor.

The rising of Sirius marked the beginning of the sweltering heat in July and August. Its effects are commemorated again and again in ancient poetry. Perhaps the Celtic word *Syr* gave this constellation its name. The Arabs called it *Suhail*, "Brilliant Star." Hindus called it *Sukra*, after the rain god. It was considered by many cultures to have a baleful influence.

Eternally in pursuit of the constellation Lepus, the rabbit, Canis Major was associated with many hunters and their dogs in the Greek canon. Some saw it as one of Actaeon's dogs and some saw it as Maera, the dog that faithfully told Erigone of her father Icarius' death (see Boötes). Others saw the constellation as Laelaps, the magical hound given by Minos to Procris (the daughter of Erechtheus, the king of Athens), who eventually gave it to her husband, Cephalus. (Because Zeus admired Laelaps so much, he put it in the sky.) This dog had been given to Procris along with a spear, and neither weapon nor dog could miss its prey. On one occasion, Cephalus tested his wife's fidelity. He disguised himself and tried to seduce her with many presents. She succumbed, and when he revealed himself she ran away to the mountains in shame. He carried on an affair with Eos (the dawn), by whom he had a son.

Procris found Cephalus again and went hunting with him without his recognizing her. He coveted

her miraculous hound and spear and had soon seduced her (the prospect of obtaining the miraculous gifts added to his ardor). She revealed herself as his wife, and the two adulterers were reconciled. She later grew jealous because Cephalus spent so much time hunting (with a dog and spear that never failed, one can understand why he enjoyed the sport). Through the machinations of Artemis (who was disgruntled with the couple), Procris followed her husband hunting one day. When she heard Cephalus call to "Aura" to come and refresh him, she grew enraged and made a noise in the bushes. Thinking that there was an animal in hiding, Cephalus threw the magic spear, and that was the end of Procris. "Aura" was simply the name of the wind. Laelaps, the infallible dog, was elevated to the heavens and chases a hare that can never be caught.

If this constellation is one of Actaeon's dogs, it is one that turned on its master. Actaeon had the misfortune of accidentally seeing Artemis, the vir-

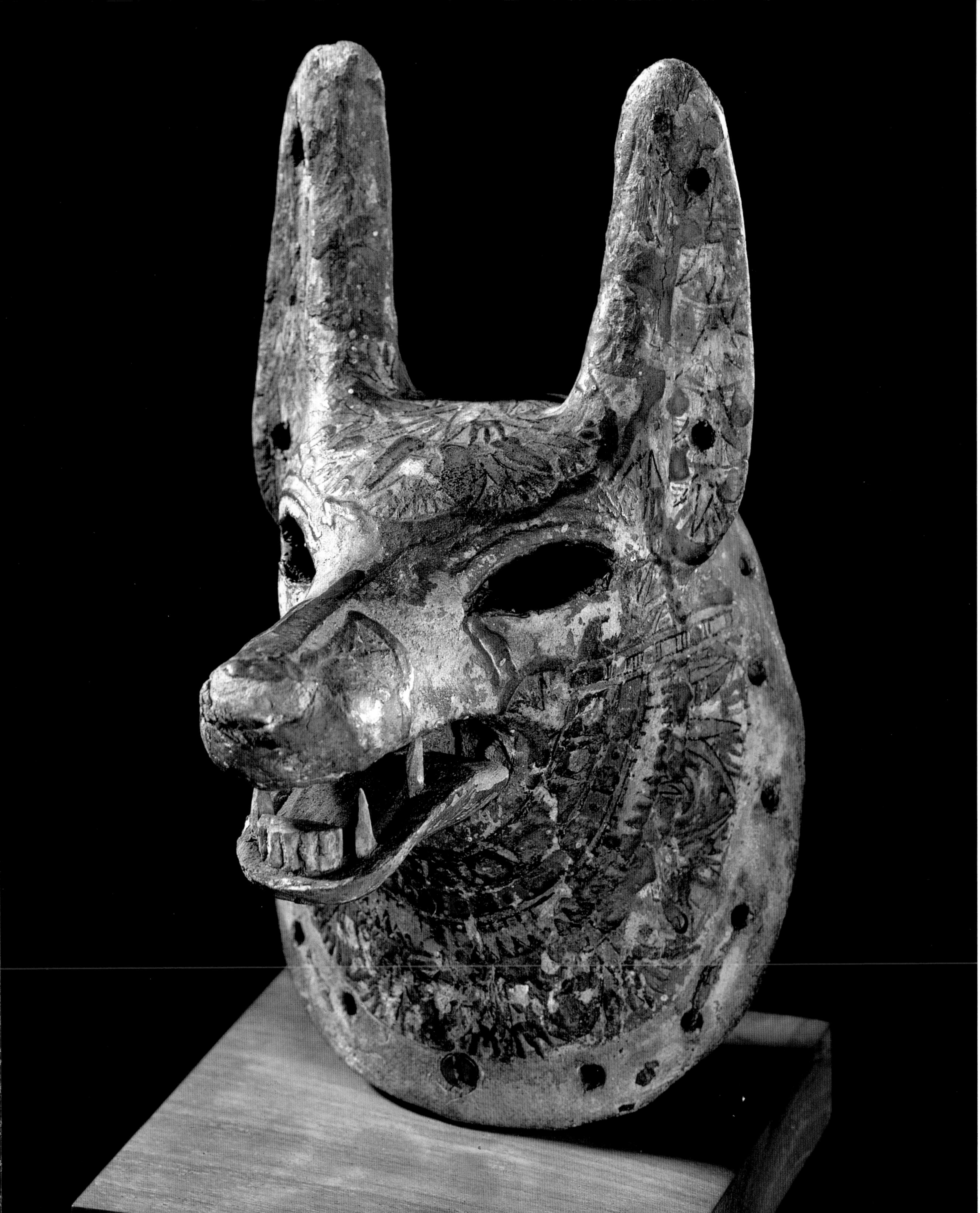

gin goddess of the hunt, as she bathed naked in a woodland pool. She was so angry she turned the hunter into a stag, and Actaeon was torn apart by his own dogs. They did not recognize him, so they kept searching for their master. They finally came to Chiron, the wise centaur who had taught their master. He made a statue of Actaeon and that was the only way he could quiet the distraught hounds.

Italy, Portugal, France, and Germany all share the Greek perception and call this constellation the dog. The Arabs also called it a dog, no doubt from their communication with Greece and Rome.

SIXTEENTH-CENTURY PAINTER FRANCESCO MAZZOLA, KNOWN AS IL PARMIGIANINO, DEPICTED THE FATE OF ACTAEON AFTER HE WAS TURNED INTO A STAG BY ARTEMIS AS PUNISHMENT FOR HAVING SEEN HER NAKED. TRAGICALLY, ACTAEON WAS EVENTUALLY DEVOURED BY HIS OWN HOUNDS.

The Sumerians use these stars along with those of Argo Navis to form a group called *Ban Kak Si Di*, or "Bow and Arrow." Parallels are found in Iran, China, and Egypt. The Chinese have named others of its stars "Soldiers' Market" and "Wild Cock." The Hindus called it *Mrigavyadha*, "Deer-slayer" or *Lubdhaka*, "The Hunter," who shoots an arrow (the belt of Orion) into the body of the criminal Praja-pati. It was also seen as one of the twin watchdogs of the Milky Way. In northern mythology, the constellation was viewed as *Greip*, a dog in the myth of Sigurd. Bible lore identifies it as the dog of Tobias.

CANIS MINOR

Rising before Canis Major, this constellation is the little dog that runs before its companion. It has some of the same associations mentioned in Canis Major. The Egyptians regarded it as a guard dog that heralded the season of flooding with its bright star Procyon (literally, "that which precedes the dog"). This star was also identified with Anubis. To the Greeks, it was associated with Actaeon, Maera, and the second hound of Orion. Canis Minor might also represent the dog that Helen lost; she asked Zeus, her father, to commemorate the dog for her. Helen was the beautiful woman whose face launched a thousand ships at the beginning of the Trojan War, which was fought to return her to her husband, Menelaus—and restore Greece's honor—after she was abducted by the Trojan prince Paris.

For the Arabs, the stars of Canis Minor are part of the gigantic Asad, or lion, that dominated the sky for desert nomads. To Christians, it was the Paschal Lamb. The Chinese saw it as *Nan Ho*, "The Southern River." They identified one star as *Shwuy Wei*, "A Place of Water." These designations may be due to its proximity to the Milky Way.

There is an Arabic love story associated with this constellation. Two sisters, al-Ghumaisa and al-Shira, fell in

love with al-Jauzah (represented by Procyon, Sirius, and Orion or Canopus, respectively). Al-Jauzah was on the other side of a great river (the Milky Way), and only one sister was able to reach him, so she is called "She who has passed through" whereas the other is "She who weeps."

THIS SEVENTEENTH-CENTURY MINIATURE FROM THE COURT OF MALWA DEPICTS HANUMAN AIDING BRAHMA IN ONE OF THE SUPREME DEITY'S ADVENTURES.

Indians named Procyon after the monkey-god Hanuman, a powerful and popular god that had counterparts in China and Japan. In India, the monkey was as sacred as the cow.

The mythical adventures of Hanuman are widely recounted in the *puranas*, sacred poems that described the lives and exploits of the Hindu gods.

Κέντανρος

CENTAURUS

As mentioned above, the centaur Chiron was the tutor of many Greek heroes, including Theseus, Achilles, and Jason (see Argo Navis). Chiron taught Asclepius his medical arts. He is also called the father of astronomy. He was of the race of centaurs for whom this constellation is named. Chiron is depicted carrying a spear, about to attack the constellation Lupus (the wolf). Others see him carrying a thyrsus (a staff topped with a pine cone or with a bunch of grapes), engaging in some rite along with the wolf.

Centaurs, like satyrs, are composite creatures—in the centaurs' case, half-man and half-horse. The top half was a human torso, including arms. According to legend, the first centaur was born from the union of Ixion with a cloud shaped like Hera. Centaurs dined on raw flesh, and in general were an uncivilized bunch—lusty, boisterous, and crazy about wine. Aside from the centaurs Chiron and Pholus, centaurs were considered wild, even dangerous.

Chiron and Pholus came from different sets of parents. Chiron was the son of Philyra and Cronus; Pholus was the son of Silenus and the tree nymph Melia. These two were similar, however, because both were civilized centaurs. As noted, Chiron was widely sought as a tutor. Studying with him was like going to Trinity in Ireland, Cambridge or

Oxford in England, or Berkeley or Harvard in the United States. In fact, time with Chiron was an ancient Fulbright award given for excellence. He taught the arts of civilization, which included reverence for the gods, the art of healing, and details about star lore. Apollo and Artemis had been his teachers.

Heracles was staying with Pholus and asked the centaur to open a large jar of wine that belonged to the centaurs in common. Pholus hesitated, but since he was a good host, finally

AMONG THE MOST FAMOUS CENTAURS WAS NESSUS, WHO WAS RESPONSIBLE FOR THE DEATH OF HERACLES. IN THIS PAINTING BY GERMAN ARTIST FRANZ VON STÜCK, HERACLES UNLEASHES AN ARROW INTO NESSUS' BACK AS THE RANDY CENTAUR ATTEMPTS TO CARRY OFF HERACLES' DEIANEIRA.

consented. The other centaurs became very angry that their wine had been drunk, but Heracles held them at bay, killing many of them. Pholus died in an accident, mortally wounding himself as he attempted to bury a fellow centaur. His generosity toward Heracles earned him a place among the stars.

Some of these centaurs fled to Chiron, who lived near Mount Pelion, but Heracles pursued them. Heracles was shooting arrows at them, during which onslaught Chiron was wounded.

Chiron was suffering so much from this wound (the arrows were dipped in the blood of the Hydra) that he agreed to exchange his immortality with Prometheus so that the centaur could die and thereby escape the agony of his wounds. Before Prometheus could be freed, another soul had to be given to Hades, who was agreeable to this arrangement. When Chiron died, Zeus immortalized the centaur, who was a bright light for many, with this constellation.

Chiron is similar to Heracles in having a bestial side and yet being a source of civilization. Heracles cleared the world of monsters and made it safe for humankind, but part of his nature is itself monstrous. Chiron has the form of a beast but acts in a civilized fashion, whereas Heracles has the form of a man and the passions of a beast (rather like the Sumerian Gilgamesh and Enkidu). In a sense, this duality parallels human nature, which has both civilized and animal drives—what Freud called the superego and id. Plato, in the dialogue *Phaedrus*, proposed a model of the soul that featured a charioteer (rationality) driving two horses (passions), one of which struggled to go up (representing such "good" passions as bravery), and one of which struggled to go down (representing such base passions as lust and gluttony). It is possible that Freud developed his model

ALTHOUGH THE CENTAURS WERE IN GENERAL A ROWDY BUNCH WITH EXCEPTIONALLY POOR MANNERS, CHIRON WAS WISE, INSIGHTFUL, CALM, AND WIDELY RESPECTED. HE EMBODIES THE HARMONIOUS RELATIONSHIP BETWEEN HUMANITY AND NATURE; IT IS IRONIC THAT HERACLES, WHOSE ANIMAL NATURE RAN STRONG, SHOULD FATALLY WOUND THIS LEGENDARY TEACHER. IN THIS ROMAN WALL PAINTING FROM HERCULANEUM, CHIRON TEACHES THE YOUNG ACHILLES.

from Plato's model. The centaur represents this dual nature with his half-animal form, and Heracles embodies the duality in his actions.

The Arabs used some of the stars of this constellation to make *Al Kadb al Karm*, "The Vine Branch." Some Christian peoples saw it as Noah, and others as a representation of Abraham and his son Isaac.

It should also be noted that Crux, or the Southern Cross, was identified by Ptolemy as part of Centaurus. It is said to have been called the Southern Cross by Royer by 1679, but it had been noted by Bartschius and Caesius earlier in the seventeenth century. This majestic constellation lights up the southern sky, and many voyagers took reassurance from it. Its five stars appear on the postage stamps (and many of the state flags) of Brazil.

The star Alpha Centauri is famous because it is closest to our sun. The Egyptians considered Alpha Centauri sacred, and oriented temples toward it. The Chinese called it *Nan Mun*, "The Southern Gate." With Beta Centauri, it forms a line that points to the Southern Cross. Various peoples have named these stars. In Australia, the aborigines saw them as the Two Brothers, who killed Tchingal with the lance of the Southern Cross. In South Africa, they were "Two Men Who Were Once Lions."

COMA BERENICES

his constellation not only has been called Berenice's Hair, it has also been called Ariadne's Hair (*coma* means "hair"). The Arabs called it the lion's tail. It has also been seen as the threads that Virgo spun or a sheaf of wheat. The Greeks thought that it represented the caduceus of Hermes. Some saw it as a cluster of ivy.

The most common tale with regard to this constellation, however, is about Berenice, the daughter of the king of Cyrene, who was married to Ptolemy III of Egypt. While Ptolemy was away waging war against Syria, Berenice ensured his safety by cutting off her long beautiful hair and dedicating it to Arsinoe Aphrodite at Zephyrium. The locks disappeared, however, and the astronomer Conon came up with the explanation that it was Aphrodite herself who turned the locks into a constellation. Ptolemy returned home safely.

Christians call this constellation "The Veil of Veronica," probably because the Herodian Beronica has a Latin name that is equivalent to Berenice ("v" and "b" are closely related). Some Christians saw it as *Flagellum*, "The Whip," the Latin word from which the English word *flagellate* is derived, which describes the instrument used to whip Christ.

The early Arabs say this as *Al Haud*, "The Pond." The Chinese had various designations,

THE HAIR HAS LONG BEEN IDEALIZED AS ONE OF THE MOST SENSUAL PARTS OF THE HUMAN BODY—IN MYTH AS WELL AS IN THE ARTS (AS IN *THE BRAID*, PAINTED BY FRENCH MASTER PIERRE-AUGUSTE RENOIR IN 1884).

such as *Chow Ting*, "The Imperial Cauldron of the Chow Dynasty."

Common to most of these interpretations is that these stars are taken to represent something fine and flowing. This constellation is a fine network of sparkling stars, and its beauty has fascinated many people over the generations, including Alexander Pope, who wrote "The Rape of the Lock," a parody of Berenice's noble deed.

CORONA AUSTRALIS

This is the southern crown of stars. It has been called Centaur's Crown because centaurs often wore a crown. Since it is near Sagittarius, it is sometimes said to be his crown; it may also represent the arrows that he shoots. This constellation was also called Ixion's Wheel (Ixion was the father of the centaurs). It may be the crown that Dionysus placed in the sky to honor his mother, Semele.

Some Arabs called it "The Tortoise." The Chinese also saw a tortoise (*Pee*). Other Arabs called this constellation "Woman's Tent," and still others *Udha al-Naam*, "The Ostrich Nest." It is said that the ostriches, figured by the constellation known to the West as Sagittarius and Aquila, would fly from the nest and drink from the Milky Way.

Christians called this "The Crown of Eternal Life," and a biblical association is "Diadem of Solomon." Because of the fact that most observers saw here a circle in the sky, the constellation was associated with circular objects that had importance in various cultures.

Στέφανος
πρῶτος

CORONA BOREALIS

It is likely that this magnificent crown of the North—rather than the Corona of the South—is Ariadne's Crown. It has brilliant streamers while Corona Australis has none. Since it is also brighter, Corona Borealis is the candidate for most of the ancient myths concerning a crown. Thus, it has been called the Crown of Vulcan, the Crown of Amphitrite, and the Cretan Crown (because of its association with Ariadne).

Ariadne was the beautiful daughter of Minos, king of Crete. She fell in love with Theseus when he came to kill the Minotaur, the monstrous son of Pasiphae and the Cretan bull. By accident, Minos' son was killed by Athenians, and as a punishment he required seven sons and seven daughters to be sent as a tribute from Athens every nine years. These sacrificial victims were fed to the Minotaur, who lived in the labyrinth constructed for him by the great craftsman Daedalus. It was a place of winding passages where one was sure to get lost; even if one escaped the Minotaur, which was unlikely, one would die from starvation looking for a way out. Ariadne helped Theseus by giving him a ball of yarn, which he unraveled behind him as he looked for the monster. After he killed the Minotaur, he was able to retrace

90

his steps. He escaped and took Ariadne with him, but ungraciously abandoned her on Naxos. This is the subject of many operas, including *Ariadne auf Naxos*, by Richard Strauss, and an earlier opera by Claudio Monteverdi that features a moving aria, "Arianna's Lament" (*Arianna* is Italian for Ariadne). Even though she wept floods of tears, she was still beautiful. She caught the fancy of Dionysus, with whom she lived ever after. The crown that Dionysus

gave her is the one that gleams forever in the heavens, a token of their love.

In another version of this myth, Minos challenged Theseus by throwing a ring into the ocean and demanding that the young hero retrieve the bauble. Theseus dived into the ocean, where Poseidon, the god of the sea and Theseus' father, saw to it that the young man was welcomed in the depths. Dolphins escorted Theseus to the palace of the

Nereids, where he was not only given the ring, but a crown (which is now in the stars). Theseus gave this crown to Ariadne when he married her. Ovid tells us that this crown was made by Hephaestus and had nine sparkling jewels, combined with gold.

Ariadne's name is related to words meaning "very bright" or "very holy." This etymological evidence suggests that at some point Ariadne was probably an important goddess—comparable to Cybele and Demeter, powerful earth goddesses.

The shape of this constellation is so suggestive that many different cultures have developed similar—if not identical—interpretations. Some Arabs called is *al-Fakkan*, "Bowl"; others called it a shield. The Persians saw it as a broken platter because of the incomplete circle. Christians saw it as the wreath of thorns that crowned Christ. Hebrews called it *atara*, "Crown." Australian aborigines saw it as a boomerang. The Chinese called it a cord.

The Shawnee people of North America told a story about celestial sisters who descended from the heavens in a basket and danced around a circular path while beating on a silver ball. White Hawk, a hunter, saw the sisters and fell in love with one of them. He tried to catch her, but the sisters were too fast, and they returned safe-

ABOVE: SOME NATIVE AMERICAN PEOPLES SAW THE CORONA BOREALIS AS A COUNCIL MEETING OF CHIEFS, AS ILLUSTRATED BY THIS EUROPEANIZED ENGRAVING FROM THE EIGHTEENTH CENTURY.

ly to heaven. Then he disguised himself as a rabbit, but they were again too fast for him. Finally he disguised himself as a mouse and was successful in making one of the sisters his wife; she, however, longed to return to heaven and join her sisters. One day, she made a basket and incanted a spell to bring her back to heaven, but she wound up in the wrong place in the sky. She became Arcturus in Boötes rather than rejoining her sisters in the Corona.

Other Native Americans saw this circle as a council meeting of chiefs, with the small central star the servant preparing the food. As mentioned above, some Native American peoples saw Corona Borealis as the cave from which a bear emerges each spring, beginning a celestial chase (see Ursa Major). Arcturus represents the owl in this myth.

The Celts saw this constellation as Caer Arianrod, "The House of Arianrod"; the resemblance of the name *Arianrod* to *Ariadne* is obvious. Furthermore, Arianrod, or Ethlenn, was a daughter of royal blood—her father was the Fairy King—just as Ariadne was the daughter of a ruler.

Jewels, flowers, and maidens are the most frequent associations made with regard to these stars (which appropriately grace the sky with their eternal light), but there is a tremendous variety of interpretations for this shining circle.

91

Κόραξ

CORVUS

This constellation is identified with the crow, which according to Greek myth was once a snow-white bird, the favorite of Apollo. One day, the bird took to tattling, and told Apollo that his beloved Coronis (whose name means "crow") had dallied with the youthful Ischys (whose name means "strong"). Coronis was pregnant at the time, but this did not stop Apollo from exacting a dire vengeance: he (or his sister Artemis) shot her dead, but saved the child, Asclepius. Hermes delivered the child from her womb while her body lay on the pyre. Asclepius was delivered to Chiron, who taught him all the arts of healing. Apollo missed Coronis immediately, but it was too late to

change her fate. Instead he turned the crow black for its trouble. As Ovid writes,

Because of his tattling tongue,
His color which was white, now is white's opposite.

Corvus is located near Virgo, and this may be the maiden about whom the crow told stories. Others say the crow was turned black by Apollo because he did not peck out Ischys' eyes. Coronis coupled with Ischys because she thought that Apollo would get tired of her, particularly as she aged. So she chose a mortal as her mate, fearing an immortal lover.

Asclepius was such a good physician that he eventually was able to raise the dead. Many complaints about the use of these powers—especially from Hades—came to Zeus' attention. To put an end to this upset in the order of things, Zeus struck Asclepius down with lightning and then restored him to life. Zeus finally put the images of Asclepius and the serpent (Ophiuchus) among the stars.

Still other myths state that Apollo turned the crow black because the bird tarried on a tree when he was supposed to fetch water for a sacrifice. The crow was attracted to some figs, so he perched on the tree waiting for them to ripen. He returned to Apollo with a snake in his mouth, lying about the delay and blaming it on the snake. The crow was cursed by Apollo with an unquenchable thirst. It was said that Apollo illustrated this by placing the constellation of the crow next to Crater, the bowl, and Hydra, the water snake, to torment the thirsty crow.

ABOVE, LEFT: As Apollo looks on, his son Asclepius is instructed by the wise centaur Chiron in this Roman painting. ABOVE, RIGHT: On the bottom of a beautiful ancient Greek cup, Apollo—with his treasured lyre—sits with his wayward crow at his side.

Another version relates that Athena, in response to Coronis' plea for help, turned the girl into a crow to enable her to escape Poseidon. Elsewhere it is written that Apollo himself took the shape of a crow during the fight with Typhon, the gigantic fire-belching monster defeated by Athena and Zeus.

Paralleling the Greek interpretation, the Hebrews called this constellation "The Raven," and the Chinese saw it as "The Red Bird." Some of the stars were interpreted by the Chinese as part of the "Imperial Chariot," which rode on the wind. Some Arabs saw these stars as part of the rump of the gigantic celestial lion, others saw it as a camel, and others a tent. To the Hindus, these stars were part of the hand of the large *Praja-pati* (*Brahma*, Lord of Creation). Christians saw several shapes in this constellation, including Noah's raven, which found land before the dove but failed to return (for which the raven may have been turned black).

93

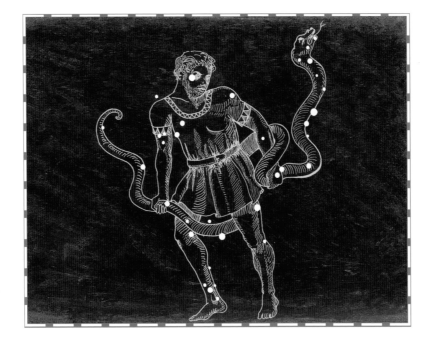

OPHIUCHUS AND THE SERPENT

This constellation is next because it is so closely associated with Asclepius. Ophiuchus means "he who holds the serpent," and that is how he is depicted. He is standing on a scorpion, another poisonous creature, symbolizing (as Heracles does) humankind's mastery of the wild. Ophiuchus could in fact represent Heracles; Hera sent two snakes to strangle Heracles when he was in his cradle. A powerful baby, Heracles was able to kill the snakes with his bare hands. Heracles also overcame the Hydra and Ladon, the dragon that

OPPOSITE: JEALOUS BECAUSE ZEUS FATHERED THE HERO-TO-BE WITH ANOTHER WOMAN, HERA SENT TWO SNAKES TO KILL THE INFANT. ALREADY IMMENSELY POWERFUL, HERACLES HAD NO PROBLEM KILLING THE SNAKES WITH HIS BARE HANDS, AS IS CLEAR IN THIS ROMAN WALL PAINTING FROM POMPEII.

guarded the golden apples of the Hesperides. (Draco and Hydra, however, have their own constellations. We have already seen the importance of Draco in myths of creation; Freud would point out the significance of the snake, particularly as the symbol of the phallus.)

Historically, physicians are depicted holding the caduceus, the staff entwined by two snakes; thus, this figure may be Asclepius, who was taught by Chiron to be a healer (see Corvus). Then again this figure may be Hippocrates of Cos, another candidate for "Father of

Medicine." The poison of snakes was used in a homeopathic way in medicines. With regard to the *chakras* in Indian lore, as investigated by Joseph Campbell, the snakes are associated with powerful forces of life.

Robert Graves associates the name Asclepius (and also the names Ischys and Ixion) with mistletoe, which is a symbol of generative and healing power. Sir James Frazer equated mistletoe with the golden bough that Aeneas carried for protection in the underworld, which makes it a symbol of life amid death (illustrated in nature by the fact that when the oak's leaves fall, mistletoe, a parasitic shrub, thrives). Druids would cut off the mistletoe from the tree in an act symbolic of castration. And to this day, the Dionysian aspects of the mistletoe survive in its being used as a license to kiss.

There are many other candidates for the mythical sources for Ophiuchus, including Cadmus (who was changed into a snake), Jason, Aristaeus (who pursued Eurydice and caused her death by snakebite), and Laocoön (who was killed along with his sons by twin snakes when he tried to warn the Trojan people about the Trojan Horse).

THIS DETAIL OF THE CON-STELLATION OPHIUCHUS CLUTCHING THE SERPENT WHILE STRADDLING SCORPIO IS TAKEN FROM A 1469 MANUSCRIPT OF *PHAENOMENA*, A BOOK MADE BY ARATUS OF SOLI (C.315–240B.C.).

The Arabs saw this constellation as *al-Raudah*, or "The Pasture." Some stars represented the boundaries of the pasture, and the enclosed stars represented a shepherd, his sheep, and his dog. Christians associate this constellation with Saint Paul, and the Maltese Viper, Aaron (whose staff became a snake), Moses, or Saint Benedict. Julius Schiller first estsablished the association with Saint Benedict to commemorate the founder of the Benedictine order, who fostered and preserved learning, as did Aesclepius/ Ophiuchus. Some Chinese societies saw these stars as "The Duke," or a mast; others named the stars after some early feudal states. Some of the stars were part of *Tien Kiang*, "The Heavenly River." Other stars were perceived as a series of shops, a market tower, or even a special district in China. These associations range from the divine through the noble to the very secular.

It is fitting that a healer find his name immortalized in the heavens and that humankind's aspiration to tame nature (and to overcome threats to human life in the form of disease and so on) be commemorated. Perhaps this constellation symbolizes the struggle of good against evil and perhaps of humankind against death itself (just as the Virgin Mary is represented standing on a snake to denote death's defeat).

Κρατήρ

CRATER

Crater (a crater is a mixing bowl in which the Greeks mixed wine with water) is another constellation with a suggestive shape that has led many cultures to interpret it similarly. In the context of the Greek mythological canon, it represents (amoung other things) a means of punishment, filled with water that Apollo's tattling crow (see Corvus) is longing to drink but can never reach. Hydra guards the bowl, which is resting on its tail. The crater may have been invented by Oenopion, the son of Ariadne and Dionysus.

The Sumerians called this constellation "The Cup of the Serpent." The Greeks called it "The Crater of Dionysus," and sometimes of Apollo; additionally, the Romans attributed it to Hercules, Achilles, Dido, and Medea. Some Greeks saw it as a cinerary urn, and still others as a water bucket.

Another story from the Greek canon that could be connected with Crater concerns a king called Demophon. During his reign, a plague struck the land; consulting the oracle, Demophon was told that a noble maiden had to be sacrificed each year for the health of the city. Each year, lots were drawn to see whose child would be sacrificed, but Demophon exempted himself from the lottery. A noble called Mastusius objected, and for this his own daughter was sacrificed, with no lots drawn. Mastusius seemed to be reconciled with Demophon over the years, but the aggrieved Greek nev-

er forgot the king's rash sentence. One day, Mastusius invited Demophon to dinner. The king, who was busy at that moment, sent his daughters before him to the feast, and Mastusius killed them. The vengeful Mastusius served Demophon their blood mixed in a crater with wine. When Mastusius announced what he had done, he was drowned in the harbor, and the crater was thrown after him (the harbor was then called "crater" and the sea "Mastusius"). The crater was elevated to the sky as another moral lesson, one often repeated in Greek tragedy: those who perform evil deeds will consequently suffer evil.

SEVERAL CULTURES INTERPRETED THE CONSTELLATION CRATER AS A DRINKING VESSEL OF SOME SORT; THE PERSIANS SAW IT AS A WINE JUG. THIS FRESCO FROM LATE-SIXTEENTH-CENTURY IRAN SHOWS A MAN POURING WINE FROM JUST SUCH A VESSEL.

Many drinks were mixed in a crater—by a variety of cultures: for instance, soma, the divine drink that restored Indra, the Vedic sun god, for his yearly fight during the summer solstice against Vritra, the serpent of darkness. This drink was directly associated with Soma, the Hindu god of the moon.

The Jews called this constellation *cos*, meaning "cup." The English saw it as a "two-handed pot" The Arabs saw it as a stall, a jar that stored wine, or a basin. Christians saw it as the "cup of Christ's passion," or the wine cup of Noah, the cup of Joseph, one of the jars at Cana, or even as "The Ark of the Covenant." The Chinese instead saw it as a Heavenly Dog.

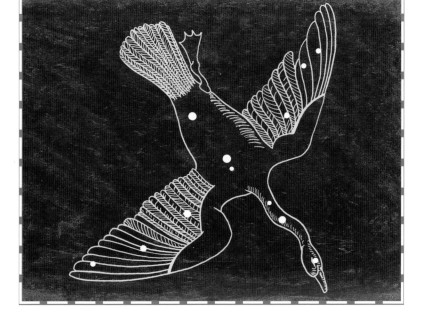

Κύκνος

CYGNUS

The constellation Cygnus, located near Lyre, is generally seen by Western cultures as having the shape of a swan. The swan is the form that Zeus assumed when he seduced Leda. Leda gave birth to the divine Helen, whose beauty led to the Trojan War. Leda also bore to Zeus Pollux, and to Tyndareus, her husband, she bore Clytemnestra and Castor. Pollux agreed to share his immortality with his twin brother Castor, so they alternate days in heaven with days in Hades. The zodiacal constellation Gemini is named after them.

Zeus also took the form of a swan in order to seduce Nemesis. Zeus, as a swan, asked Aphrodite to disguise herself as an eagle and pursue him. Nemesis took pity on the fleeing swan, and held it close to her breast during the night to protect it (and in so doing allowed Zeus into her bed). The chase of the eagle and swan now goes on for eternity in the heavens, commemorating this event.

Others say that Nemesis fled from Zeus, taking the form of a goose and hiding from him. He then took the form of a swan and was able to mate with her. It is said that the egg of this union was given to Leda to hatch, and that, after it hatched, it bore Helen and Pollux.

The beautiful Helen, married to Menelaus, king of Sparta, was an instrumental figure in the events leading up to the Trojan War. Helen was abducted by Paris, a Trojan prince. Some say Helen went with Paris willingly, persuaded by Aphrodite (who had promised her to Paris as a reward for judging the goddess of love the most beautiful in a contest of looks with Hera and Athena). Eventually, Helen was reunited with Menelaus, and they both were transported to the Elysian fields.

Ultimately, the Trojan War can be traced to the beauty contest involving Hera, Athena, and Aphrodite. As mentioned above, the judge was Paris. In order to persuade the mortal to judge her the fairest, each goddess offered him a reward: Hera offered him power and territory; Athena offered wisdom and wealth; and Aphrodite offered him love and the most beautiful woman in the world, Helen. Paris chose Helen, and the fate of Troy was sealed. Paris returned to Troy with his prize, and the Spartans were not long in following. After a ten-year siege that culminated in the deployment of the Trojan Horse, which held the fighting men of Sparta inside, Troy fell and Paris was killed.

Another Greek myth relates that Cygnus, the son of Apollo and Hyria, drowned himself in a lake after Phylius, a hero who was in love with him, accomplished some "impossible" tasks that Cygnus had set him; rather than subject himself to the hero's affections, Cygnus committed suicide. Cygnus' mother drowned herself as well, and both were transformed into swans. Another version of the same myth depicts Cygnus as the son of Poseidon; when Cygnus was killed by Achilles during the Trojan War, his father had him transformed into a swan. Yet another myth says that Cygnus was a king of Liguria and the friend of the foolhardy charioteer Phaethon. Zeus killed Phaethon with a thunderbolt in order to stop the devastation the young man was causing in the run-

ABOVE: TO THE CHINESE, SOME OF THE STARS OF CYGNUS MAKE UP PART OF THE CONSTELLATION CALLED *TANG SHAY*, "THE DRAGON."
OPPOSITE: THE CONSTELLATION CYGNUS MAY REFER IN PART TO THE FORM TAKEN BY ZEUS WHEN HE SEDUCED LEDA. THIS PAINTING BY RENAISSANCE MASTER LEONARDO DA VINCI IS PERHAPS THE BEST-KNOWN DEPICTION OF THIS SEDUCTION.

away chariot of the sun. Cygnus mourned his friend so much that he was changed into a swan; Apollo gave Cygnus the swan a beautiful voice.

The first documented mention of the swan's song is in *Agamemnon*, the play by Aeschylus: Clytemnestra, who has just murdered her husband and his mistress Cassandra, the prophetess of Apollo, compares her to a dying swan who sings sorrowfully before she dies. This image is adopted by Plato in the *Phaedrus*, where he declaims the superiority of swans to men in foretelling their death, which the birds herald by singing more beautifully than they ever did in their lives. Robert Graves claims that swans conveyed royal souls to a northern Paradise, and in other myths they are associated with death.

The swan constellation is in the shape of a cross, so it also has the name "Northern Cross." Christians took it as an obvious symbol of Christ. It has been called the true cross that Helena, Constantine's mother, found. It is interesting that this constellation relates to such opposites as Helen and Saint Helena.

The Arabs call this constellation "The Hen," "The Partridge," or "The Carrier Pigeon." The name of its bright star Deneb comes from *Al Dhanab al Dajajah*, which is Arabic for "The Hen's Tail." Other Arab cultures called it *Al Fawaris*, "The Riders." To the Chinese, some of the stars of the Shepherd (see Aquila) are to be found in this constellation. The Chinese named individual stars in this constellation after a city and a storehouse for carts; some of the stars formed a part of *Tang Shay*, "The Dragon."

DELPHINUS

This constellation is in the shape of a dolphin, an animal sacred to Dionysus. It is in the portion of the sky called "The Sea" by the Greeks. Dolphins swim freely in the Mediterranean and are well known for their intelligence and friendliness toward humans. The dolphin is said to have helped Poseidon when he courted Amphitrite, for which the animal was rewarded by being placed in the sky. A dolphin also helped Arion, a famous poet, by carrying him home safely after his own crew had robbed him and then tried to drown him. Arion asked the sailors if he could sing one last song before being thrown overboard: dolphins heard and came to his rescue as he bobbed in the ocean.

Arion arrived home at Corinth before the thieves returned. When the criminals landed, they were apprehended and executed. It is said that Apollo put both Arion's lyre and the dolphin in the heavens to commemorate this deed.

Dolphins figure prominently in other Greek myths as well. One such tale relates that some pirates kidnapped Dionysus and took his ship; struck by the god's beauty, they decided to sell him into slavery. They soon regretted it. Dionysus caused ivy to grow around the ship, transformed the oars into snakes, and changed himself into a lion. Various animals roamed the decks until the pirates threw themselves overboard. Once they struck the water,

the pirates were changed into dolphins. This series of events is said to account for the dolphin's remarkable intelligence.

The Chinese saw this constellation as *Tien-Kion*, "Celestial Stable." They called some of the individual stars in the grouping "The Gourd" or "Rotten Melon." The Indians called it a sea serpent. Some Christians saw the constellation as the cross of Jesus; others saw it as Leviathan, the

THE BOTTOM OF THIS GREEK BOWL, WHICH DATES FROM THE SIXTH CENTURY B.C., ILLUSTRATES THE VOYAGE OF DIONYSUS DURING WHICH THE ENRAGED YET COMPASSIONATE GOD OF WINE TRANSFORMED A BAND OF PIRATES INTO DOLPHINS.

great fish that swallowed Jonah; and still others (including Julius Schiller) saw it as the water pots of Cana.

Most Arabic interpretations of the constellations are particular to the desert environment they come from; hence there are many camels represented in Arabic constellations, including this one. Some Arabs, however, saw this constellation as a collection of pearls instead.

ERIDANUS

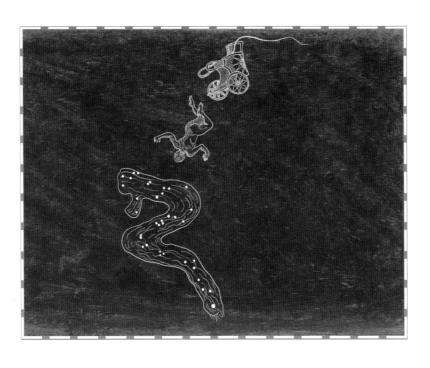

This constellation is likened to a river, and flows in the portion of the heavens that was called "The Sea" by the Greeks. Resembling a gigantic horseshoe, Eridanus is the longest constellation. Originally a mythical river, Eridanus came to be associated with many actual rivers, including the Nile, the Euphrates, the Phasis, the Quadalquivir, the Ebro, the Rhine, and the Rhone. Pherecydes, a sixth-century B.C. Greek author of cosmogonic myth, and later Roman authors identify this river with the Po. It has even been called the river of Orion. Perhaps the enormous constellation represents a stream that flows into the Mediterranean Sea from Europe in the northwest.

Or it could represent Homer's "river of the ocean," which he claimed encircled the earth. The star Sirius is near this constellation; since the appearance of Sirius signals the yearly flooding of the Nile, it was natural for the Egyptians to associate this heavenly river with the Nile.

The Greeks claimed that the constellation represented the river into which Phaethon fell after being struck dead by Zeus' thunderbolt. Since Phaethon was the son of a god (Helius), the gods commemorated him by placing the river in the sky. Phaethon's sisters, the Heliades (daughters of Helius), were turned into poplars; it was said that their tears became drops of amber. Some of the rivers

associated with the Eridanus were the routes along which the amber trade flowed, which reflects the tale of the Heliades. Some sources state that the sisters of Phaethon were punished because they did not ask their father's permission before they turned over the chariot and horses to their foolhardy brother.

Christians associated this constellation with the Jordan or with the Red Sea. The Chinese called one star *Yuh Tsing*, "The Golden Well," and others *Tien Yuen*, "The Heavenly Park."

ALTHOUGH THE ERIDANUS WAS A MYTHICAL RIVER, MANY ACTUAL RIVERS—INCLUDING THE NILE—HAVE BEEN ASSOCIATED WITH IT THROUGH THE CENTURIES. THIS COLOSSAL MARBLE STATUE FROM THE VATICAN IS A REPRESENTATION OF THE NILE; NOTE THE SPHINX PERCHED ON THE FAR RIGHT.

Both are associated with water. The Arabs called some of the stars "Ostrich" and "Ostrich Nest." Jews saw twins in two pairs of stars within the larger star grouping.

As this constellation demonstrates, the world's cultures populated the heavens not only with people and animals, but with beautiful scenery and objects as well. The bright sparkle of the heavenly Eridanus may not only be the sunlit surface of the stars, but the honeyed gleam of amber.

Λύρα

LYRA

This beautiful constellation commemorates Orpheus' lyre or possibly the lyre of Amphion. Some early depictions presented the instrument as if it were held in the claws of an eagle. The lyre itself was invented by Hermes. While just an infant (albeit a precocious one), the trickster god stole some cattle from Apollo. He then strung some cow's guts across the shell of a turtle and found it made a wondrous sound—wondrous enough, in fact, to enchant Apollo and secure his forgiveness for the young god's theft. Apollo carried the instrument as a favored symbol of the music he

OPPOSITE: THIS NINETEENTH-CENTURY PAINTING BY GOTTLIEB SCHICK SHOWS APOLLO AMONG THE SHEPHERDS, HIS EVER-PRESENT LYRE UNDER HIS RIGHT ELBOW.

inspires. "The Homeric Hymn to Hermes" tells the whole story. (There is also a wonderful modern version of the myth presented in *The Trackers*, a play by Tony Harrison, that was inspired by fragments from the *Ichneutae*, by Sophocles. Harrison depicts Apollo as a selfish bully who tries to corner music entirely for himself and not share it with the masses.)

The Greeks also called this constellation "Turtle," referring to the origin of the instrument. Persians saw it as the lyre of Zurah. In Bohemia, it became *Hanslicky na Nebi*, "The Violin of the Sky." The early Britons identified it as

Talyn Arthur, "King Arthur's Harp." For the Irish, the lyre is as much a symbol of their nation as the dragon is the national emblem for the Chinese.

Orpheus was given the lyre by Apollo, and found he could use its musical power in a number of ways. For instance, playing the lyre, he was able to tame wild animals and move the rocks and trees to tears. Orpheus met and fell in love with the maiden Eurydice. Just after he married her, she was fatally bitten by a snake as she picked flowers. Orpheus went to the underworld to try to win her back, charming the spirits by playing his lyre and singing. Persephone, in particular, remembered her own experience of being ravished (by Hades) as she picked flowers. Persephone pleaded with her husband, Hades, to permit Eurydice to return to the land of the living. The god of the underworld relented, allowing Eurydice to follow Orpheus back to earth on the condition that Orpheus not turn back to see her before they arrived. The musician failed the test: longing for his bride, he looked back prematurely, only to see her fade back into Hades again. In grief at his loss, Orpheus returned to earth and played the most mournful music ever heard, causing the very rocks to weep. He was happened upon by the Maenads, who—unable to get his attention—tore him limb from limb. In some versions, Orpheus was said to have infuriated the Maenads because of his sexual inaccessibility; in fact, he is said to have introduced homosexuality to Thrace. At any rate, after being torn apart, his head was thrown into the Hebrus river. The head eventually arrived at the isle of Lesbos, where it began prophesying at a temple of Dionysus (who also had been dismembered).

Seventeenth- and eighteenth-century opera composers preferred happier endings to their dramas. At the end of Monteverdi's opera *Orfeo,* Apollo consoled Orpheus with the promise that he and Eurydice would live together in the stars. Later, Gluck also wrote a magnificent opera on this subject, and the outcome was even happier: Orpheus looked back, but he did so in response to Eurydice's own pleas. The gods admired his fidelity and decided to allow the two lovers to be reunited in spite of the musician's violation of their command. Now the heavenly lyre shines as a fiery commemoration of Orpheus and Eurydice's love.

One can see in the myth of Orpheus an analogy with the sun. If Orpheus represents the sun, then Eurydice is his bright counterpart, the dawn, who disappears as soon as he waxes in strength. She returns each day.

One of the brightest stars in this constellation is Vega, which is identified with She-niu, the weaver, and her beloved shepherd Altair who meet once a year, crossing the Milky Way (see Aquila). The Indians called this star *Abhijit,* "The Victorious One." This was a star of good omen signaling the defeat of the Asuras by the gods (the triumph of good over evil). For many years, they saw the constellation as an eagle. The Arabs also saw Vega as an eagle; whereas with the Arabs the wings are perceived as folded, however, to the Greeks Aquila is in flight, with wings spread. Christians saw Lyra as King David's harp, and it was also thought to represent the manger where Christ was born. The Peruvians identified it as a multicolored ram that guarded flocks.

Some say that the Lyre was put in the heavens to entertain Heracles, whose constellation is nearby. Just as Orpheus' lyre music made the rowing of the *Argo* easier during the quest for the Golden Fleece, so perhaps were Heracles' labors alleviated by its emanations. The lyre is also a symbol of the arts; it is interesting to note that, although the gods may have invented the instrument, mortals perfected its use.

Ὀυρίον

ORION

rion is one of the most famous Greek constellations: the three bright stars in the belt are often the only part of a constellation that people can identify. Orion was a great hunter: he is usually depicted holding a club or a sword that he swings at the bull, Taurus. He is also near a unicorn and a rabbit, so he does not lack for game. Finally he has Canis Major, his trusty dog, nearby.

Orion was the son of Euryale and Poseidon or Hyrieus (actually he may have had several fathers). His mother may have been Gaia, so if his father were Poseidon, he was a combination of the traits of the earth and the sea;

some versions of his tale depict him walking on water, a gift from his father. Other versions depict him as being so tall that when he walked along the ocean floor, his head rose above the waves.

It is said that Zeus, Poseidon, and Hermes were visiting Hyrieus, who gave them all the hospitality he could offer. The gods asked him what he wanted in return, and he said a son. The gods then urinated into the skin of the ox that they had been fed, and Hyrieus was told to bury it. (Some versions state that Hyrieus himself was told to urinate in it.) From that ox-skin, Orion was born. His name is related to the Greek word for "urine." He was also very handsome.

Orion went to Chios and fell in love with Merope, the daughter of the king. In return for Merope's hand, the king requested that Orion slay all the wild beasts on the island. When the slaughter was over, however, the king reneged. Orion, not unlike Heracles in being impatient and hot-tempered, drank too much one night and raped Merope. Oenopion put out Orion's eyes as punishment. Hephaestus' apprentice Cedalion guided the blind hero to Delos, where he could be cured by Helius, the sun. In ancient Greece, the sun was thought to create sight. Eos, the dawn, saw the handsome Orion and seduced him. It is said that she blushes when she rises because she remembers his embraces.

Ultimately, Orion was killed by Artemis, either because he challenged her hunting abilities or tried to rape some maidens who followed her (see Pleiades). Some say that he tried to rape Artemis herself, who sent a giant scorpion after him in revenge. This scorpion stung him mightily, eventually killing him, and was rewarded by being transformed into a constellation.

Other versions tell the story differently: Apollo, protecting his sister's honor lest she succumb to Orion's attractions, sent the scorpion. Apollo even went so far as to trick his sister into aiming an arrow at a black spot swimming in the ocean that

THIS UNATTRIBUTED SIX-
TEENTH-CENTURY PAINTING
OF THE FONTAINEBLEAU
SCHOOL DEPICTS PERHAPS
THE GREATEST—NOT TO
MENTION MOST IRRITABLE—
HUNTER OF THEM ALL,
ARTEMIS. SHE WAS RESPON-
SIBLE FOR THE UNHAPPY END
OF SEVERAL MORTAL HEROES
UNFORTUNATE ENOUGH TO
RUB HER THE WRONG WAY.

happened to be Orion. She was duped and was the inadvertent source of Orion's death. His constellation was mentioned in Homer's writings. Other versions of the myth state that on one occasion Orion was hunting with Artemis and boasted that he would kill every animal on earth. Gaia overheard him and sent a giant scorpion up to kill him. It stung him and he died, and both were placed in the heavens—not only as a warning to others but as a tribute to Mother Earth. The chase continues: whenever Scorpion rises, Orion sets, so the scorpion continues to be victorious.

The Egyptian gods Osiris and the star Isis were also seen in the constellation Orion and the star Sirius. The Egyptians also saw Orion as Horus, in a boat, followed by a cow (Sirius), also in a boat (Isis was often represented with cows' horns, possibly referring to her relation to the crescent moon). Indians saw this constellation as the god Praja-pati in the form of a deer. The deer pursues a roe, his daughter Rohini (represented by the star Aldebaran), but the hunter Lubdhka (Sirius) prevents him from carching the roe by shooting an arrow (the three stars of Orion's belt) into the deer. The Jews had various names for this constellation, from "Impious" to "Foolish" to "Violence" to *Gibbor*,

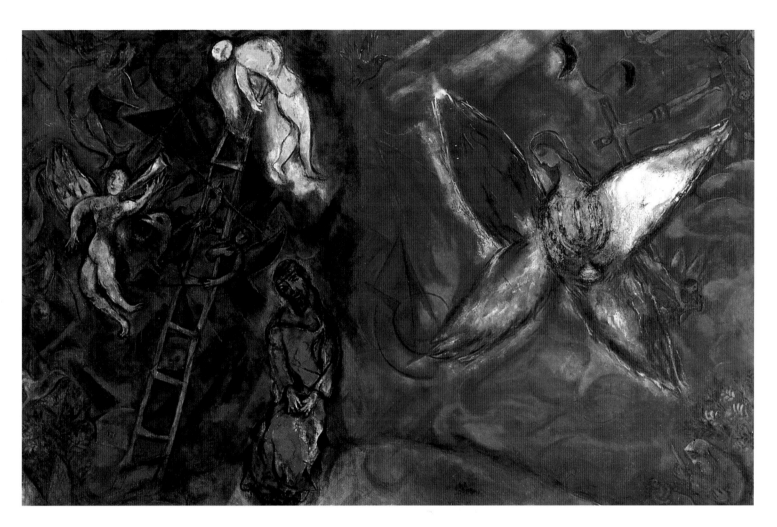

"Giant" (recalling the foolish Nimrod, who rebelled against Jehovah). Christians saw it as Joshua, Jacob, or Saint Joseph. Some Christians saw the three stars of the belt as "Our Lady's Wand," while others saw the grouping as the Three Magi.

The Irish called this constellation *Caomai*, "The Armed King." A modern appellation dubs it "California of the Sky." In the nineteenth century, some French called the stars of the belt "Napoleon"; the English promptly retaliated, calling the stars "Nelson." French farmers called the three stars "The Rake," and in Germany the

SOME PEOPLE SEE THE CONSTELLATION OF ORION, WHOSE BELT MAKES HIM ONE OF THE MOST VISIBLE IN THE NIGHT SKY, AS JACOB. AN OLD TESTAMENT FIGURE, JACOB WAS THE THIRD OF THE HEBREW PATRIARCHS (WITH ABRAHAM AND ISAAC) AND IS THE FATHER OF THE TWELVE SONS WHO WOULD IN TURN FATHER THE TWELVE TRIBES OF ISRAEL.

same three stars were "Three Mowers." (This is proof, perhaps, that constellations often take the shape of what one wants to see, or what one is familiar with; in a sense, they are the Rorschach blots of the sky.)

The Chinese pragmatically called the belt stars "Three Stars." They had many other names for the other stars in Orion, including "Three Flags," "Golden Well," "Head of the Tiger," "Sharp Edge," "Middleman," and even "Punishment." Some Arabic cultures saw a belt, a string of pearls, or nuggets of gold. The Hindus saw the three stars as a three-jointed arrow. Some Native Americans saw the sword of Orion as an arrow aimed at three mountain sheep (the belt stars). Other Native Americans saw other kinds of game in these stars: antelope, deer, and sheep. Some aborigines in Australia saw these stars as three men in a heavenly canoe; others saw them as three young men trying to attract some girls (the Pleiades). In Greenland, the constellation was *Siktut*, "Seal Hunters," who were lost while hunting and transposed to the heavens. The Norse saw the stars in the belt as *Fiskikallar*, meaning "Staff"; Scandinavians called it *Frigge Rok*, "Frigg's (or Freya's) Distaff," from which she spun the thread to create the clouds that float over Midgard, where the mortals dwell. Other Scandinavians called the constellation "Kaleva's Sword," and still others "Tavern."

Betelgeuse, the constellation's main star, which is located in Orion's shoulder, gets its name from the Arabic name *Ibt al-Jauzah*, "The Armpit of He Who Is in the Center." It gleams bright orange. The star Bellatrix, "Warrior Woman," is on the left shoulder of Orion. People from the Amazon River called Bellatrix "Young Boy in a Canoe." Some Arabic cultures called it "One Who Roars," referring perhaps to the lion skin that is sometimes depicted in Orion's left hand. Rigel, another famous star from this constellation, is the brightest in this grouping; the name comes from the Arabic word *Rijl*, from *Riji Jauzah al Yusra*, "Left Leg of the Jauzah." Some stars were the Herdsman of the Jauzah, complete with camels. The Norse considered it the thumb of the giant Orwandil. The other thumb, which had

THIS MESOPOTAMIAN RELIEF DATES FROM THE SECOND OR THIRD MILLENNIUM B.C. AND MAY REPRESENT A WRESTLING MATCH BETWEEN ENKIDU AND GILGAMESH.

been frozen, was cut off by Thor; it became the star Alcor in Ursa Major.

Orion has also been associated with the Sumerian epic of Gilgamesh, the legendary king of Uruk. He abused his power and lived in a dissolute way, seducing the maidens of the land. The people complained. Elsewhere, a double, Enkidu—who was covered in hair—was created to provide a rival for Gilgamesh. The sun-god Shamash used a priestess of Ishtar to seduce Enkidu and bring him away from the wild country in which he thrived. She took him to Uruk. He learned the ways of civilization, eating cooked food for the first time. He rubbed off his hair and was very handsome. He was shocked to hear of Gilgamesh's wanton ways, and he stopped the profligate as Gilgamesh was on his way to an erotic rendezvous and wrestled with him. They became fast friends and undertook various adventures. They first tried to slay the giant Humbaba. Enkidu tried to talk Gilgamesh out of this, but Gilgamesh said that if he could not obtain immortality (and what mortal could?), the least he could do would be to achieve great deeds (similar sentiments are found in Homer's *Iliad*, which may have been influenced by this epic: Achilles and Patroclus resemble Gilgamesh and Enkidu). After a great struggle, the friends were able to kill Humbaba. Then they purified themselves.

Gilgamesh was so handsome that Ishtar pursued him. Gilgamesh refused her indignantly, pointing out the disastrous ends that her lovers suffered. Because she was rejected, she begged Anu, her father, to send the celestial bull against them (the zodiacal constellation Taurus is near this constellation).

112

Gilgamesh and Enkidu slew the bull and threw the pieces at Ishtar in defiance. Ishtar was rightly furious and demanded that the gods avenge her: one of the duo would have to die to compensate for her loss. Enkidu died and Gilgamesh suffered leprosy. Gilgamesh mourned at his friend's side for many days, until a worm crawled out of his nose.

Gilgamesh went to the desert and continued his mourning, growing his hair long and wearing a lion skin. He was terrified by death. He decided to consult Utnapishtim, his great-uncle (and analogous to Noah), to find out how he could become immortal, since the gods had made Utnapishtim himself immortal. On the way, he had to overcome scorpion men, go through great darkness, and was rewarded by a vision of paradise—a forest where the trees gleamed with brilliant multicolored gems.

Siduri, a divine maiden, tried to dissuade him, saying that man should be satisfied with enjoying music, dance, celebrations, and a loving wife and children—but these were not for our hero. He continued his treacherous voyage over the sea of death, until he finally met Utnapishtim. Utnapishtim also tried to discourage him, saying that all men must die, that only very few were exempted: in his case, it was for his good and pious deeds. Utnapishtim cured Gilgamesh's leprosy and decided to test Gilgamesh by getting him to stay awake for seven nights. He failed miserably, not even being able to stay awake for one night. But Utnapishtim told him about a tree that grew branches that would make him immortal if he could keep a branch with him. Gilgamesh succeeded in finding the tree and acquiring

THIS DETAIL FROM AN EARLY EIGHTEENTH-CENTURY STAR MAP SHOWS ORION SURROUNDED BY LEPUS AND TAURUS.

the branch, but he set it down when he took a swim, and a serpent swallowed it.

Gilgamesh was forced to accept his mortality. He buried his beloved friend. He even persuaded Nergal, the god of the dead, to let him talk to his friend once more. Enkidu told Gilgamesh that if a man dies in battle and is buried with honor, then that person has some comfort, but the one whose body is abandoned in the fields has no rest.

This tale contrasts civilization with the life of the primitive and concludes, as does the *Iliad*, with an affirmation of mankind's mortality. Man's life is symbolically traced in this epic: we are all savages as children, and when overcome by disease and old age, we return to a primitive state, as Shakespeare states us in the speech about the "Seven Ages of Man," from *As You Like It*.

The Iliad and the tale of Gilgamesh celebrate not only life, but also death achieved in the midst of youth and glory. These young glorious heroes have found their way to the stars in Perseus, Heracles, and Orion. It is rare to find the aged immortalized in the Greek and Western myths about the stars. For such representations it is necessary to refer to the heavens as seen in China, where old age is venerated.

As Thomas Kinsella puts it, describing an old man looking at himself in a mirror:

> *In slow distaste,*
> *I fold my towel with what grace I can,*
> *Not young and not renewable, but man.*

Hitch Your Wagon

to a Star

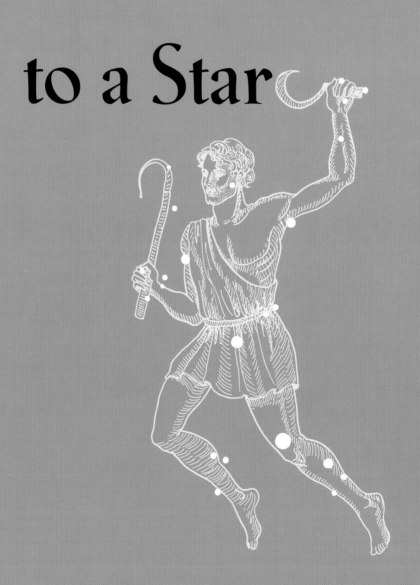

Clearly, there are major differences in the interpretations of star myths throughout the world, and at the same time many similarities. The similarities can be attributed to the more-or-less fixed patterns of the stars and also to the wanderings of various peoples. There are nevertheless particular characteristics in the stories told by shepherds, who see sheep and pastures, and by fishermen, who see fishes and rivers. In the north, there are stories about snow (in Sweden, the Milky Way is Winter Street, and in Siberia, a ski track left by a god); in the tropics, there are stories about water, rain, and floods (in Sanskrit, the Milky Way is "The Bed of the Ganges"); and stories about winds and dust are told in the mountainous areas (the Peruvians see the Milky Way as star dust).

The Chinese differ the most from Westerners in what they see; they routinely placed their bureaucracy in the sky, including all the various classes, from king to peasant. They added gods, animals, objects, and abstract principles, such as *Ten Li*, or "heavenly wisdom." Confucianism led to an ordered society that has found its way into the heavens. The constellations of China do not tell the stories of violence that the Western ones do, but reflect the order and control of their society. They have stories of love, such as that of the Weaver (the star Vega) and the Shepherd (the star Altair), rather than Western tales of rape (for instance, those surrounding the constellations Orion and Cygnus). There is also an acceptance of the natural that is not

THIS FIFTEENTH-CENTURY WALL PAINTING BY RAFFAELLO ILLUSTRATES THE HEAVENS AND THE CONSTELLATIONS AS PART OF A GREATER WHOLE, WHERE UNSEEN HANDS (THE WOMAN FIGURE AND THE CHERUBIM) ARE AT WORK.

as idealizing as in the West: thus "Piled-up Corpses" (Algol in Perseus) can be found in the heavens, as can the stars called "Heavenly Sewer" (Cetus). Jesuits brought stories from the West, and so some constellations have similar names, but if one digs deeply, one usually finds another story that explained a particular constellation originally.

The Arabs have different representations, which are usually nonhuman in accordance with certain precepts of Islam after the seventh century A.D. But these constellations, too, have taken over some these common Western images. One also finds mundane representations, such as of camels and the paraphernalia associated with living in desert climes.

Native Americans often found tales of the hunt in the heavens. They also put some of their gods, who were so important in governing the weather, in the heavens. The Polynesians often had tales of fishing and voyages (the Milky Way is a big shark). African myths speak of hunting and the animals that are indigenous to their various countries. Indians see the universe as resting first upon a snake, then a turtle, and then four elephants (all indigenous animals). One tribe of Native Americans, the Chumash, have myths about the Sky Coyote in a yearly gambling match with the sun; if he wins, the earth flourishes, whereas if the sun wins, there is drought and death. Again, these tales are populated by local animals. The perception among the Australian aborigines of the Corona Borealis as a boomerang is another illustration of the elevation of day-to-day paraphernalia to heavenly status.

The Jews see their tribes and their symbols in the sky. Christians see the twelve apostles in the constellations of the zodiac, and recount Christian stories where they can, taking whatever in the Greek canon that resembles some Christian account.

The Greeks have put their heroes in the sky (for example, Perseus) and sometimes their criminals (Cassiopeia) and sometimes the method of punishment (Ixion's wheel in Ursa Major). Their passions are embodied there, with tale after tale of anger and rape—and also some tales about noble achievements. The violence of the tales contrasts with the more restrained stories that China has put in its heavens. Some of the Greek myths are tales of human life and death, and of the alternation of the vital crop in its cycle of life and death.

Celtic interpretations usually relate to heroes—legendary, epic, or historical. The Indians placed their gods in the sky, especially those associated with myths that deal with humanity's survival—for instance, Indra's victory over Vritra, representing the triumph of light over dark. On the more practical side, India is a country of many jewels, which have made their way into their heavens.

So we conclude our brief tour of the heavens. We have witnessed the struggles of heroes and the loves of men and gods commemorated for all time in these shining memorials. Saint-Exupéry located the Little Prince in the heavens after the little inter-

AS THE PRIMARY GREEK DEITY OF THE ARTS, ESPECIALLY MUSIC, APOLLO HAS MANY COUNTERPARTS IN MYTHOLOGICAL CANONS AROUND THE WORLD; MORE THAN ANYTHING ELSE, IT IS THE CREATIVE IMPULSE ITSELF THAT LINKS TOGETHER MEMBERS OF OTHERWISE ENTIRELY DIVERSE CULTURES.

galactic traveler left earth. In the heavens, humans share immortality with the gods. The threatening monsters they conquered and the beasts that helped them are still to be seen at their side. Human life continues in a stellar form. Some chases—and some loves—will continue for eternity.

We can apply Keats' words from "Ode on a Grecian Urn":

> Bold lover, never, never canst thou kiss,
> Though winning near the goal—yet, do not grieve;
> She cannot fade, though thou hast not thy bliss,
> For ever wilt thou love, and she be fair!

The constellations shall always be fair, and they will no doubt continue to inspire great passion in the peoples of the world. In the heavens, human beings achieve the ultimate catharsis—through the constellations and the myths attributed to them. These groups of stars can be the loci of prayers and the source of great happiness—indeed, the presence of the stars makes it a joy to be alive. The stars are also our protectors. For every threat (scorpion or bear), there is a hunter or a hero to save us. Our life unfolds with the stars, which themselves announce the seasons that punctuate our existence. Among the stars, there is always the promise of life and a new dawn, even if preceded by a desperate struggle. In the theater of the sky, these dramas are replayed every night, with new installments that unfold throughout the year.

117

Bibliography

Allen, Richard Hinckley. *Star Names: Their Lore and Meaning*. 1899. Reprint, New York: Dover Publications, 1963.

Freud, Sigmund. *The Interpretation of Dreams*. 1900. Reprinted in *Great Books of the Western World*, edited Robert Maynard Hutchins.

Graves, Robert. *The Greek Myths*. 2 vols. 1955. Reprint, New York: Penguin, 1986.

Krupp, E.R. *Beyond the Blue Horizon: Myths and Legends of the Sun, Moon, Stars, and Planets*. Oxford: University Press, 1991.

Lévi-Strauss, Claude. *Structural Anthropology*. Translated by Clair Jacobson. New York: Basic Books, 1963.

Lloyd-Jones, Hugh. *Myths of the Zodiac*. London: Duckworth, 1978.

Sesti, Giuseppe Maria. *The Glorious Constellations: History and Mythology*. Translated by Karin H. Ford. New York: Harry N. Abrams, Inc., 1991.

Martin, Martha Evans, and Donald Howard Menzel. *The Friendly Stars: How to Locate and Identify Them*. 1907. Reprinted and revised, New York: Dover Publications, 1964.

Ovid. *The Metamorphoses of Ovid*. Translated by A.E. Watts. San Francisco: North Point Press, 1980.

Photography Credits

AKG London: pp. 53, 67, 74, 84, 87, 100, 103

Archive Photos: p. 18

Art Resource, N.Y.: pp. 32, 111; © Archivi Alinari: p. 44; © Borromeo: p. 82; © Werner Forman Archive: pp. 16, 21 both; © Giraudon: pp. 11 bottom, 14, 17, 20, 45, 46, 59, 78, 79, 110; © Lauros-Giraudon: pp. 12, 13, 23; © Erich Lessing: pp. 15, 36, 41, 50, 56, 68, 107, 112; © National Museum of American Art, Washington, D.C.: pp. 34, 57; © Photo Nimatallah: p. 27; © The Pierpont Morgan Library: p. 96; © Scala: pp. 5, 8, 24, 25, 29, 37, 38, 40, 48, 51, 61, 63, 64, 65, 66, 69, 71, 72, 73, 76, 80, 85, 90, 93 both, 95, 101, 105, 115, 116; © SEF: p. 98; © Tate Gallery, London: p. 31

E.T. Archive: pp. 22, 42; © Victoria and Albert Museum: p. 19

Constellation illustrations by Emilya Naymark

North Wind Picture Archives: pp. 10, 52, 60, 117

Stock Montage: p. 91; © Charles Walker Collection: pp. 9, 113